LLEWELLYN'S

Little Book of

YULE

© Tymn Urban

J ason Mankey is a third-degree Gardnerian High
Priest and helps run two Witchcraft covens in
the San Francisco Bay Area with his wife, Ari. Jason
is a popular speaker at Pagan and Witchcraft events
across North America and Great Britain and has
been recognized by his peers as an authority on
the Horned God, Wiccan history, and occult influ-
ences in rock and roll. He is the channel manager
at Patheos Pagan and writes there at *Raise the Horns*
and for *Witches & Pagans*.

LLEWELLYN'S
Little Book of
YULE

JASON MANKEY

LLEWELLYN PUBLICATIONS
WOODBURY, MINNESOTA

FIRST EDITION
Second Printing, 2021

Cover cartouche by Freepik
Cover design by Shira Atakpu
Interior art elements designed by the Llewellyn Art Department

Llewellyn Publications is a registered trademark of Llewellyn Worldwide Ltd.

Library of Congress Cataloging-in-Publication Data

Names: Mankey, Jason, author.
Title: Llewellyn's little book of Yule / by Jason Mankey.
Description: First edition. | Woodbury, Minnesota : Llewellyn Worldwide,
[2020] | Includes bibliographical references. | Summary: "Filled with
dozens of magical exercises, tips, recipes, crafts, spells, and rituals,
this pocket-sized guide shares everything you need to make your Yuletide
memorable and enchanting"—Provided by publisher.
Identifiers: LCCN 2020017393 (print) | LCCN 2020017394 (ebook) | ISBN
9780738763071 (hardcover) | ISBN 9780738763149 (ebook)
Subjects: LCSH: Yule (Festival)
Classification: LCC BF1572.Y85 M36 2020 (print) | LCC BF1572.Y85 (ebook)
| DDC 394.261—dc23
LC record available at https://lccn.loc.gov/2020017393
LC ebook record available at https://lccn.loc.gov/2020017394

Llewellyn Publications
A Division of Llewellyn Worldwide Ltd.
2143 Wooddale Drive
Woodbury, MN 55125-2989
www.llewellyn.com

Printed in China

To my brothers, Chuck, Dason, and Derick:

thanks for all the holiday memories!

Also to my cats, Princess, Evie, and Summer: I don't apologize

for dressing you all up as elves over the years.

Contents

✳

Exercises

Tips

INTRODUCTION

I remember one Christmas Eve vividly, even though it was nearly forty years ago. We were at my grandparents' house, snug and comfortable in their back room. There was a fire in the hearth and about a dozen stockings hanging above it on the mantel. For the night before Christmas, it was rather quiet, with just the drone of the television and a few bits of conversation spread out among the twelve people there.

Suddenly the silence was broken by a loud "ho!" as Santa entered the house from the front door with a bag of presents slung over his back. He made his way quickly to the back room as my three brothers and I all began to hysterically yell "Santa!" Since it was Christmas Eve, Santa was all business and took charge of the situation rather quickly, telling us that we'd all been good that year and deserved a little extra something for our efforts.

Unlike the Santa at the mall, this Saint Nick knew us all by name, which is tricky when one of your brothers is named Dason. (Naming us Dason and Jason was not planned. Technically he's my stepbrother, but we grew up together, so he's my brother.) One by one, Santa called to each of us, and when we approached, he handed us a gift. These weren't just any gifts, either. They were perfectly tailored to what we were all interested in at the time. My brothers got three different sets of Matchbox cars, each set reflecting them individually. I got a set of little green army men, but with Japanese soldiers, which have always been nearly impossible to find.

His task completed, Santa wished us all a good night and prepared to leave. My brothers and I weren't quite ready for the visit to be over, though, so we followed him to the front door of the house and listened intently for the sound of a car, hoping to catch our parents in the act of tricking us. But there was no sound. Santa simply left the house and was swallowed up by the night—or picked up by reindeer.

Santa paid us this visit when I was in the fourth grade, about the age when most kids stop believing in Kris Kringle. That night I searched my grandparents' house high and low for a Santa suit and went through my immediate family trying to figure out who had been playing Santa. (Who else would have known who we were? Plus, my grandparents lived in a different town than we did.) Over the ensuing years, I've asked my father several times about that particular night, and he has always told me that he doesn't know who was behind the beard—unless it was Santa Claus, of course.

Today, the word *Yule* is used in a variety of different ways. For many, it functions as a synonym for *Christmas* and has been used that way for over seven hundred years. Modern Witches and Pagans use Yule to signify the Winter Solstice, a practice that date backs at least seventy years. The ancient Norse most likely celebrated Yule over a period of several days near the Winter Solstice. At my house we celebrate Yule as an entire season, one that encompasses a wide range of holidays and traditions.

In the Middle Ages, it became popular to call the winter holiday season *Yuletide* or *Christmastide*. Yuletide began on Christmas Eve (December 24) and lasted until Epiphany (January 6). It was a period full of heavy drinking, gift-giving, religious services, and customs that could be traced all the way back to the time of the Roman Empire. Given how the holidays of late autumn and early winter all sort of blend together in a blur of green and red lights, I think of Yuletide today as beginning on Thanksgiving and extending through Epiphany, and in some places beyond even that.

My own journey as a spiritual person has included many of the holidays that make up today's Yuletide. I grew up in a Christian household, celebrating Christmas with my family in the Methodist Church. In my early twenties, I embraced Modern Wiccan-Witchcraft and began celebrating the Winter Solstice both alone and with other Witches. In my late twenties, I began throwing some of the best New Year's Eve parties in the world (or at least in my neighborhood). In recent years, I've embraced

even more Yuletide holidays, such as Krampus Night and Twelfth Night.

When I began writing this book, I knew it would be about more than just the Winter Solstice and Christmas, because I love *all* of the holidays that make up Yuletide. My goal was to write a book for everyone who cherishes the diversity found in our early winter holidays. This book is full of holiday history, arts and crafts related to the season, and even several recipes. There are well-known holiday traditions in this book, and a few holidays many people have probably never heard about.

This book also embraces magic, and many of the activities included here are magical in nature. Modern Witches use magic as a tool to transform their lives and take control of their circumstances. In many ways, magic is about invoking a certain feeling or emotion, and a lot of the magic in this book is about making Yuletide the best it can be. If you aren't familiar with magic, don't let it scare you, and if you're a longtime magic user, I hope the spells in this book make your Yule even more bewitching.

The fact that this book includes magic shouldn't be much of a surprise. Yuletide has been full of magic and the miraculous for thousands of years. December has long been home to elves, talking animals, virgin births, and plants that might help one steal a kiss. To me, all of those things are pretty magical, and they are the types of things that are celebrated by many people only at the start of winter.

When I look at the world today, it's downright mundane most of the year, but that all changes at Yuletide. We decorate the world with lights to fight off the darkness, and everything just seems a little more joyous than usual. People are often nice to one another for no particular reason, and there's a spirit of generosity and goodwill that is largely absent from our society today most of the time. Knowing that there could be a Christmas card tucked in between the bills and advertisements makes routine activities such as checking the mail enchanting.

Perhaps the most wondrous thing of all about the holiday season is that people have been celebrating it in the Western world for literally thousands of years. Our ancient ancestors observed the sun and the night sky with a keen eye and knew when the solstices and equinoxes occurred, but there was something very different about Yule. They *celebrated* in December, and they did so with lots of wine, cider, and beer, all while decorating with holly, ivy, and evergreen branches. Our celebrations today aren't exactly the Roman Saturnalia, but they do share some commonalities and likely will continue to do so long into the future.

Winter celebrations are also surprisingly resilient. Despite what some people believe, there is currently no "War on Christmas," although there have been wars against the holiday in the past. These wars generally pitted Christians against one another, one group determined to celebrate with as much joy as they could muster and another group dead set against a holiday with heavy pagan overtones. The fact that Yuletide has continued to thrive in such conditions is a testament to the magic and awe that accompany it.

Growing up in the Methodist Church, I always found Advent season to be a welcome change of pace from the doom, gloom, and boredom that often accompanied church services. There were candlelight sing-a-longs at Christmas Eve and a "hanging of the greens" service the Sunday evening after Thanksgiving. My love for the holiday season only intensified after becoming a Pagan and adopting Wiccan-Witchcraft as my spiritual practice. So many of the Christmas traditions I grew up with were Pagan, so I kept them as a Witch, and even added new ones to the mix.

I have long loved Yuletide and was obsessed with it long before Santa showed up at my grandparents' house. My friends today often comment that it looks like "Christmas threw up all over my house" at the end of each November, and they aren't wrong. Yule does take over my living room, kitchen, bathroom, and front porch every year, and I wouldn't have it any other way!

It's my hope that this book serves as a love letter for the most magical season of all—Yuletide!—and that it brings all of you who read it closer to the traditions you cherish and honor. Whether you celebrate Christmas, Hanukkah, the Winter Solstice, Yule, Twelfth Night, New Year's Eve, or Krampus Night, I think you'll find something to love in this book.

Chapter One

FROM SATURNALIA
TO CHRISTMAS

People have been celebrating on and around the Winter Solstice for thousands upon thousands of years. While many of the traditions we associate with Christmas and Yule today are legitimately old and date back to pagan antiquity, reverence for the Winter Solstice goes back even further and predates written records. It's likely that people began commemorating the Winter Solstice as early as 10,200 BCE, which is all the way back to the end of the Stone Age.

The earliest known monument built to commemorate the Winter Solstice is the Goseck circle in Germany. Nearly seven thousand years old now, the Goseck circle is a series of rings, two of which are aligned with the sunrise and sunset on the Winter Solstice. Much more famous is the Newgrange monument in northeastern Ireland. Newgrange is a large circular mound with several tunnels and chambers within it. Built around 3500 BCE, Newgrange was designed so that on the morning of the Winter Solstice, its largest chambers would be filled with the light of the rising sun. Even today, people still visit Newgrange to view this spectacular sight, and for those unable to make the trip or get in, it is streamed live on the internet every year.

Though generally associated with the Summer Solstice today, Stonehenge also aligns with the Winter Solstice, and in ancient times this association was probably most important. Though many of the most famous monuments to the Winter Solstice from the ancient world come from Europe, there are other monuments in Egypt, Mexico, and Peru. There was something about the Winter Solstice that resonated with people all over the world.

Today we most often associate the time around the Winter Solstice with positive feelings. For many of us, it's a time for presents, giving, and holiday parties. But for our ancient ancestors, winter could be an extremely dangerous time of year. A meager harvest in the fall could mean an especially perilous winter, with little to eat. Winter weather was also dangerous, as too much snow could mean a caved-in roof or no way to get out of the house. Even during times of abundance, it's likely that our ancestors were always at least a little bit worried about the potential consequences of the winter season.

Luckily for us, the most lasting holiday traditions were generally festive ones, and the celebrations that have had the greatest impact on today's Yuletide came from the Roman Empire. The most famous was *Saturnalia*, which was a week of feasting in honor of the Roman agricultural deity Saturn (*Kronos* in Greek mythology) that took place in mid-December, from December 17 through the 23rd. Originally a one-day holiday celebrated on the 17th, Saturnalia eventually evolved into an entire week of merriment. Though historians are unsure exactly when

Saturnalia was first celebrated, it was most certainly an ongoing event by 300 BCE and lasted in official form in many places until the year 500 CE.

Saturnalia was a time for heavy drinking and for subverting the social order. Slaves were waited on by their masters, and cross-dressing was common. People decorated with candles and evergreen branches, exchanged gifts, and celebrated the returning light. Much like our modern-day Christmas, Saturnalia was a day free from work and school, and the Roman Senate was prohibited from declaring war during this holiday.

Similar to Saturnalia and occurring just a week or so later, the Roman celebration of the January *Kalends* has also influenced our modern Yule celebrations. All of the Kalends (the first day of each calendar month) were celebrated by the Romans, but the January celebrations were especially festive. Like Saturnalia, it was a time to decorate with evergreen branches and exchange gifts. The fourth-century Roman writer Libanius (314–c. 394) once commented that at the January Kalends, "The impulse to spend seizes everyone.... People are not only generous towards themselves, but also towards their fellow-men. A stream of presents pours itself out on all sides" (Forbes, *Christmas,* 28).

If this sounds similar to the modern-day celebration of Christmas, that's not a coincidence. Christians "borrowed" many of the traditions associated with Saturnalia and the Kalends. When the Roman Empire converted to the religion established by Jesus and Paul the Apostle, the candles, gifts, and evergreen branches all became part of Christmas. (It would be a few more centuries before the Christmas tree appeared.)

Christmas wasn't originally celebrated by Christians, which is not surprising since only two of the four gospels in the Bible even mention the birth of Jesus. Those two gospels, Matthew and Luke, don't even tell the same story. In Luke, Jesus is a god for the common people and is attended to by shepherds. In Matthew, Jesus is a far more "royal" ruler, and it's in his story that the Three Wise Men first show up (though the writer of Matthew never specifies an exact number of Wise Men).

The first Christian celebration to possibly commemorate the birth of Jesus took place at least two hundred years after the death of Jesus. That holiday, Epiphany (which means "showing forth"), was sometimes used to commemorate Jesus's baptism and other times his birth. (Today, Epiphany refers to the Three Wise Men visiting Jesus on

January 6, but that was not originally the case.) Christmas as the celebration of Jesus's birthday wasn't celebrated until at least the year 336 CE and might have first occurred even later than that. By the year 400 CE, Christmas and the date of December 25 had been adopted by most Christians in the Roman Empire and has been celebrated in one form or another ever since. Lacking any December traditions of their own, Christians used the trappings of Saturnalia and the January Kalends to celebrate their new holiday.

• EXERCISE 1 •
Saturnalia Wine

The Romans loved their Saturnalia wine, and while they usually drank it cold, they also enjoyed it warm (and most certainly at room temperature too!). In the first century CE, a recipe for Saturnalia wine was written down in the Roman cookbook *Apicius,* generally attributed to the Roman writer Marcus Gavius Apicius. The recipe here isn't exactly like the one found in the *Apicius* (I wanted to make things a little easier), but it's close.

To Make This Special Saturnalia Wine You Will Need:

- 2 cups honey
- 2 bottles white wine

- 2 dates or 3 dried figs or 2 tablespoons raisins
  (Choose only one of these options!)
- 2 teaspoons black pepper
- 4 bay leaves
- Several strands of saffron

Start by pouring the honey into a large saucepan and adding one cup of wine. Bring to a boil, stirring as you go. Once the honey is dissolved in the wine, add the remaining ingredients, cover, and simmer for ten minutes.

After letting the wine cool for a bit, you'll have to strain the sediment out of it. I think the easiest way to do this is by pouring the mixture into a large pitcher, using a traditional wire mesh strainer to remove any bits in the wine. Once you've strained the wine, put it in the fridge for a few hours to let all the ingredients fuse together. You can then drink it chilled or heat it back up for those cold winter nights.

✳ ✳ ✳

Today a fierce debate rages on as to exactly why December 25 was chosen as the date for Christmas. Many Christians like to argue that Jesus was literally born on December 25, having been conceived on March 25. Coincidentally, March 25 is the day they think Jesus died, and an old tradition asserts that Christian saints generally died and were born on the same date. December 25 was home to celebrations honoring the deities Mithra and Sol Invictus ("Unconquered Sun"), who were both popular when Christmas was established. I think the date of December 25 most likely has something to do with its proximity to the Winter Solstice, Saturnalia, and the Kalends, but we'll never know for sure.

Today the word *Yule* is generally used as a synonym for *Christmas* or as a term to mark the Winter Solstice among Pagans and Witches. The original Germanic Yule (sometimes spelled *Jul*) was probably more than just a day, though, and most likely commemorated an extended season from the middle of November through the middle of January. The focus of the first Yule celebrations was on feasting, especially the consumption of pork, which was considered a treat and a luxury. In addition to food and drink, Yule celebrations included candles, bonfires, Yule logs, ghost stories, and evergreen branches. Yule celebrations in Germany and Scandinavia most likely paved the way

Today the word Yule is used as a term to mark the Winter Solstice among Pagans & Witches.

for similar celebrations of Christmas, with their traditions inserted into the holiday.

As Christianity spread throughout Europe after the collapse of the Roman Empire, Christmas spread with it. Indigenous autumn and winter celebrations and customs became a part of the Christmas season, while new ones evolved as the holiday grew in popularity. During the medieval period, many old deities, fairies, and spirits were transformed into seasonal gift-givers, while the Saturnalia and Yule customs of excessive eating and drinking remained strong.

One of the most popular and enduring customs of the medieval Christmas was the *Lord of Misrule*, a figure who presided over holiday merriment and subversion in royal courts throughout Europe. If you think the holiday season is long now, it was even longer a thousand years ago among European royalty, commencing on All Hallows' Eve (October 31, Samhain/Halloween) and lasting through February 2 (Candlemas/Imbolc). During the long holiday season, the Lord of Misrule would stage card games, masquerades, and other forms of entertainment, much to the delight of those with the money and resources to indulge in such things.

Away from castles and keeps, the common folk celebrated the Lord of Misrule and Christmas too, though with less extravagance and for a much shorter period of time. The popularity that came with being the Lord of Misrule eventually led to the custom's downfall. Violence often erupted when a Lord of Misrule was being chosen, leading many castles and villages to abandon the tradition, though it would live on in other forms.

• EXERCISE 2 •
Craft a Holiday Calendar

Advent calendars are popular in many Christian households during the holiday season, and they typically count down the days in December until Christmas. The most common Advent calendars generally have a piece of candy (or other treat) included with each day. Because the extended Yule season features so many different holidays, I like to create a similar calendar every season to help me connect with those celebrations. You can include as many holidays as you wish with this project, but I usually start on Thanksgiving and go all the way through Three Kings' Day.

Instead of using candy, I like to include a small candle with every holiday (though if you have children or just like candy, it's fine to use it), along with a list of things to connect with at every holiday. You can either use candles whose colors remind you of a particular celebration or just use the same color of candle for every holiday. (White candles are generally the cheapest and most abundant type, so I tend to use those.) On each holiday you can choose to connect with specific individuals or perhaps with a certain group of people or an idea that's important to that holiday. (I've included some ideas below.)

This is a great activity for those with children, as you can use it to teach them about holidays outside your own family's traditions.

For This Project You Will Need:

- Small decorative bags/pouches, preferably in holiday colors (The exact size of the bags will depend on what you plan to put in them.)

- Glitter glue pens (or other decorative writing instruments)

- Small pieces of paper and a pen to write down things you associate with each holiday

- Heavy, decorative ribbon

- Binder clips, for clipping the bags onto your ribbon

- One candle for each bag

Start by figuring out which holidays you want to commemorate with your calendar, then write the name of each holiday on a bag with the glitter glue pens. Next, write down the things that you want to honor at each holiday on small pieces of paper. Here are the holidays I honor with my calendar, along with a few ideas to put on those pieces of paper:

THANKSGIVING: Nature spirits, Native American tribes, ancestors who celebrated the holiday

KRAMPUS NIGHT: Wild deities, teachers, the fey (or fairy folk)

SAINT NICHOLAS DAY: Norse deities such as Odin or Thor, charity, the spirit of generosity

HANUKKAH: Sophia (goddess of wisdom), freedom fighters, those lost in the Holocaust

WINTER SOLSTICE: New beginnings, the power of the sun, silence

CHRISTMAS DAY: Spirits of Past, Present, and Future; beloved dead (friends and family we've lost)

KWANZAA: Religions of the African diaspora (Voodoo, Santeria, etc.), the Underground Railroad

NEW YEAR'S DAY: Classical paganism (Romans, Greeks, Egyptians, etc.), fresh starts, New Year's resolutions

THREE KINGS' DAY: Magical ideas, astrology, compassion and mercy

Once each bag has been filled up with pieces of paper and a candle, hang your decorative ribbon in a place where you'll remember to look at it every day. (You don't want to miss a holiday!) Then clip the bags onto the ribbon in whatever order you choose. Traditional Advent calendars often switch up the days preceding Christmas, making it a bit of a challenge to find each day's treat. You can do that with this calendar or hang the bags up in chronological order (which is my preference).

At every holiday you've chosen to honor, take a moment to light the candle you placed in the bag on the appropriate day. When you light the candle, take a deep breath and pause for a few minutes to think about what that particular holiday means to you or might mean to others who celebrate it. Think of the ideas, powers, and people who should be remembered at that holiday, and hold them in your mind and heart for a few moments. If you're using the calendar with another person (or persons), reserve some time after the lighting of each candle to talk about the history of the holiday you are honoring and why it's important to others. Extinguish the candle when you're through talking about the holiday, or let it burn out on its own, provided it's being watched over.

✳ ✳ ✳

The custom of *wassailing* was a continuation of the Saturnalia custom of subverting the social order. During a traditional wassail, the poor and less fortunate would visit the homes of the rich and the nobility to ask for food and strong drink, threatening violence or vandalism if their demands were not met. As was the custom, those with wealth would invite the wassailers into their homes and serve them, which was something that happened only near Christmastime.

In the English-speaking world, Christmas experienced a sharp decline in observance during the seventeenth century. Puritan preachers began to label Christmas a "pagan" holiday (and to be honest, they weren't wrong!), and many had become concerned about the excessive drinking and violence that had come to be associated with the season. As the American and British middle classes began to grow in size and strength, many of them became alarmed by the violence and vandalism directed at them by wassailers and responded by locking their doors and ignoring much of the holiday.

Christmas never really went away during this time, but its importance began to be downplayed, and during the 1700s through much of the 1800s, schools and businesses remained open on Christmas Day. (Even today, with twenty-four-hour stores and very few vacation days for many folks, especially in the United States, most businesses are closed on Christmas Day.) Christmas remained a major holiday in much of Europe, but it would take a combination of several different factors to reignite interest in the holiday in the Americas and Great Britain.

The holiday season would probably be quite different today were it not for a poem first released anonymously in 1823 that is generally attributed to Clement Moore (1779–1863). That poem, *A Visit from St. Nicholas* (more commonly known as *The Night Before Christmas*), helped transform Christmas from a drunken revel into a children's holiday. Santa Claus existed long before Moore's poem, but his words turned Santa Claus into an American obsession every December. Moore's description of Santa

Claus the gift-giver was so popular that his version was eventually imported from the Americas and became the standard in much of Europe, pushing out other traditional gift-givers. (Don't worry, we'll get to all of them later!)

Over in Great Britain, the marriage of Queen Victoria (1837–1901) to the German Prince Albert (1819–1861) in 1840 helped pave the way for a Christmas renaissance in the British Isles. When Albert married Victoria, he brought with him Germany's love of Christmas and its traditions, including the Christmas tree, a custom that spread rapidly after its adoption by Victoria and her court. Due to the popularity of the royal family, the Christmas tree soon showed up on the shores of the Americas, where it has remained ever since.

Just a few years after Victoria's marriage, the English writer Charles Dickens (1812–1870) published *A Christmas Carol* in 1843. Dickens's novella showcased a new sort of Christmas. There was still eating and drinking, but it was all mostly benign, with no unwanted visits by wassailers or violent drunks to spoil the proceedings. He also moved much of the celebration into the family parlor, with the holiday's celebration occurring around the dinner table surrounded by close family.

It's common these days to read about Charles Dickens either "inventing" or "creating" the modern-day Christmas, and while those accolades are a bit of an exaggeration, the popularity of his work certainly helped restore the holiday to prominence. His version of Christmas was one that could be celebrated by *anybody* and was a time of goodwill and charity. Who *wouldn't* want to celebrate such a thing? Dickens's Ghosts of Christmas Past, Present, and Yet to Come became familiar harbingers of the holiday season, and Ebenezer Scrooge is one of the most well-known characters in literary history.

Moore, Dickens, and Victoria and Albert helped kick off the Christmas renaissance, and as the nineteenth century progressed, the popularity of Christmas only grew. Holiday gifts were marketed toward a growing middle class, and the holiday became more and more about giving, especially to children. The rise of leisure time also played a role, with people now having the time to utilize all of those gifts they were given at Christmas. By the end of the nineteenth century, most of the ideas and customs we associate today with Christmas had been established. Trees, gifts, stockings, Christmas dinner, and the holiday as a nationwide observance were a part of most celebrations in Europe and the Americas (and by now Australia, too).

The twentieth century would turn Christmastide into a much more diverse and robust holiday season. Traditions such as the Jewish Hanukkah rose to prominence largely due to their proximity to Christmas and the holiday season. As pagan practices were reestablished, the commemoration of the Winter Solstice (the whole reason for the season to begin with!) increased in popularity both in and out of the magical community. During the 1960s, the African celebration of Kwanzaa was established in the US and spread throughout the African diaspora.

Today, Christmas is bigger than ever, but Yuletide now offers much more than just that one holiday. November and December are full of a multitude of celebrations that I consider to be a part of the Yule season's fabric, and old Christmas and solstice practices are being reestablished in Europe and the Americas. In addition, "new" traditions continue to be invented every few years. If history is any indicator, the winter holidays are here to stay and will probably only increase in popularity.

The Many Holidays of Yuletide

Yuletide is more than just one holiday; it's a season that spans from the end of November through the beginning of January. The holidays that make up the Yule season encompass a variety of traditions and cultures. It's impossible to write about Yule without also writing about Christmas and several other holidays, because the majority of them are related and interconnected.

One thing that Christmas has proven over the centuries is that holiday traditions are portable. Things that were celebrated during the Roman Saturnalia and the Norse Yule were moved to December 25 to accommodate the needs of Christian seekers. Today, we can move traditions generally associated with Christmas back to their original spots, or to whatever holiday most resonates with us and our families. There's nothing wrong with moving Santa's day of arrival to the Winter Solstice or referring to a Christmas tree as a Solstice or Yule tree. Holidays and their extended customs exist for us!

Thanksgiving and Repose

The fourth Thursday in November is reserved for the celebration of Thanksgiving in the United States. The origins of the modern Thanksgiving celebration date back to medieval England and the celebration of *Harvest Home*, a holiday observed by local communities to commemorate a successful harvest. Today we associate Thanksgiving with the Pilgrims who landed at Plymouth Rock in modern-day Massachusetts, but that association is a modern one and didn't become popular until the end of the nineteenth century.

Thanksgiving was always an important holiday in my family, and today I celebrate it as a way to remember my grandparents. I also use it as a time to remember and honor the Native Americans who were the original people to come to the land that I call home. Long before the first Thanksgiving, people had been living in the Americas for centuries and celebrating with large feasts.

Canada also celebrates Thanksgiving, but there it's much more of an autumn holiday than an early winter one. Canadian Thanksgiving takes place on the second Monday in October and has been celebrated officially since 1879. Prior to 1957, the holiday was generally celebrated on the third Monday in October. Thanksgiving dinner in Canada looks much like its counterpart in the US, with turkey, stuffing, and mashed potatoes, though it's often consumed on the Sunday before the actual holiday.

For the last hundred years, Thanksgiving has served as the kickoff to the Yuletide season in the United States, so I think it's worth mentioning in this book. I also associate Turkey Day with two other holidays. The most important of those is *Repose*, a holiday created in the 1960s by Fredrick Adams and Svetlana Butyrin, the founders of the Pagan tradition known as Feraferia.

> For the last hundred years, Thanksgiving has served as the kickoff to the Yuletide season in the US.

Repose is generally observed on the day after Thanksgiving and honors the changes that occur in the natural world in late November. Repose can be celebrated with a traditional type of seasonal ritual or simply by leaving an offering outside for the earth and/or any nature spirits you might share your yard with. Late November tends to be radically different from late October, as the trees have usually all dropped their leaves by then and snow has yet to be a major concern.

Whether or not one goes shopping on Black Friday (the day after Thanksgiving) is mostly a matter of personal choice. But regardless of whether you choose to brave the hordes at the mall or not, the sheer amount of money being spent makes it a great opportunity to reflect on mass consumerism. Perhaps instead of going to the mall you could use the weekend to do something for a friend or family member.

• EXERCISE 3 •
Honoring the Earth at Repose

By the end of November, my garden generally lies fallow and empty, the harvest having been totally completed. But I know that below the surface, life continues to churn, and the soil we all rely on for sustenance will soon be renewed by both snow and rain—something most certainly worth celebrating! Repose offers a golden opportunity to thank the earth for her gifts, and for many Americans, its proximity to Thanksgiving reinforces such thoughts.

Even if you don't have a garden or yard, it's likely that you have a favorite patch of earth and grass somewhere nearby where this exercise can be done. Besides, we all enjoy the fruits of the earth in some way, and we don't have to grow own own food to feel a deep connection to the natural world. The earth sustains us even if we don't actively participate in her agricultural cycles.

All you need for this activity is a drink or food that you really enjoy. If you're going to give the earth a gift, it should be something more than just the leftovers you weren't planning to eat; it should be something you value. In my house that's most often wine, cider, or whiskey, and at Thanksgiving time it might include one of the leftovers I really *want* to eat.

Once you've chosen your libation, take it outside to your garden or other spot and think for a moment about what the earth has given to you this year. I always thank my garden out loud for the tomatoes, peppers, and pumpkins that grow there each year. I also thank the nature spirits that I believe inhabit my backyard for allowing me to share their space. (Even if you don't believe in nature spirits, maybe it's best to stay on their good side, just in case!)

Once I've verbalized my thanks, I pour or set my offering upon the ground while saying:

> *I thank the earth for the gifts given to me,*
>
> *The fruits of bud, blossom, leaf, seed, and tree.*
>
> *Nature spirits, you who share with us this land,*
>
> *I share with you this token from my hand.*

Accept my offering, both land and fey,

Made to you in love and joy this Repose Day!

Saints Days

Due to the popularity of Santa Claus, the most familiar saintly celebration during Yuletide is the Feast of Saint Nicholas on December 6. Especially popular in the Netherlands, Nicholas's day of commemoration often includes the passing out of gifts to children. In medieval England, it was common for young boys to assume the roles of bishops and priests in the Catholic Church on the Feast of Saint Nicholas.

Krampus Night, the celebration of the fearsome Krampus, takes place on December 5. Though not a saint, the Krampus is celebrated on this day because he has been known to assist the kindly Nicholas this evening on the saint's gift-giving rounds. In some parts of Europe, the Krampus also strikes out on his own, generally to frighten children into good behavior.

Saint Lucy's Day is held in commemoration of the Christian saint Lucy (sometimes Lucia) on December 13, which is the date of the old Winter Solstice in the Julian calendar. The most well-known celebrations of Saint Lucy take place in Northern Europe, where she is often depicted with a crown of candles encircling her head. The light and warmth of Saint Lucy's candles is a welcome sight in the cold of Nordic December. Lucy's name derives from the Latin word *lux*, which translates as "light."

Celebrations of Saint Lucy might have been inspired by the Norse sun goddess *Sol*, or *Sunna*, who was most likely celebrated near the Winter Solstice. Whether her origins lie in Christianity or Norse paganism, Saint Lucy is a comforting presence in a Yuletide with far more male figures than female ones. In Sweden, it's traditional to eat saffron-flavored buns (*lussekatter*) topped with two raisins and shaped like the letter *S* to look like a sleeping cat (the raisins being the eyes, of course).

In many parts of Europe, including Germany, Ireland, and Scandinavia, Saint Stephen's Day is a continuation of the Christmas holiday and is often recognized as a state holiday. Saint Stephen's Day commemorates the life of the first Christian martyr, Stephen, who allegedly died in the year 34 CE.

In many Protestant countries, Saint Stephen's Day was transformed into Boxing Day. Gifts given in a box were traditionally passed out to employees and service workers (such as the mail carrier) on the day after Christmas, which is where Boxing Day gets its name. In much of the United Kingdom and in Canada, Boxing Day has become a major shopping holiday, much like the American Black Friday. People head out to the shops looking for great deals after Christmas!

Yule/Winter Solstice

Yule (originally *Jol* in ancient Norse) is a timeless mid-winter tradition nearly as old as the Roman Saturnalia that was originally celebrated by the Norse and Scandinavian peoples. Depending on the source, Yule was either a two-month celebration stretching from the middle of November to the middle of January every year, a twelve-day celebration beginning on the Winter Solstice and lasting until early January, or a three-day feast beginning on the eve of the Winter Solstice and lasting until the day after the solstice. One thing we can be sure of is that the Winter Solstice itself was important to those who celebrated Yule fifteen hundred years ago.

Linguists aren't exactly sure what the word *Yule* originally signified. It has been linked to the Anglo-Saxon *hweal*, which means "wheel," and could be a reference to the sun, which was often depicted as a wheel. It might also derive from the same root word for *jolly*, which would make it particularly appropriate for the holiday season. After the Christianization of Europe and Great Britain, the word *Yule* became a synonym for *Christmas*.

Specific references to Yule in ancient (pre-Christian) literature are scarce, but it was undoubtedly celebrated. Catholic Church leaders complained about the revelry of Northern European pagans near the new year for hundreds of years. The great English historian Bede (672–735) wrote about a holiday he called *Modranect* (also spelled *Mōdraniht* or *Modranicht*, depending on the source), which translates as "Mother's Night" in Modern English.

According to Bede, Mother's Night was celebrated on December 24 (Christmas Eve) by the Anglo-Saxon pagans then living in Britain and included nighttime rituals. Modern scholars believe that Mother's Night most likely celebrated a mother goddess (or goddesses). Thanks to Bede, we can be relatively certain that an early winter holiday of significance was celebrated by Northern European pagans on or near the Winter Solstice every year.

In some ways, ancient Yule ceremonies looked much like modern-day celebrations of Yuletide. There was feasting, drinking, singing, and storytelling. Familiar holiday customs such as the Yule log and supernatural holiday beings were a part of the proceedings as well. But there was also animal sacrifice and, most likely, the anointing of statues and idols with the blood of sacrificed pigs, horses, and cows.

Though Yule as a pagan holiday was dormant for several centuries, it returned by the middle of the twentieth century. When the first book about Witchcraft as a living (and positive) tradition was published in 1954 (Gerald Gardner's *Witchcraft Today*), it included part of a ritual commemorating the Winter Solstice and it called the holiday *Yule*. Modern Witches have been celebrating this *sabbat* (the term for a Witch holiday) and using the word *Yule* for it ever since. Yule is one of the eight sabbats on the *Wheel of the Year*, a term Witches use to describe the annual change of the seasons. Many Witches and Pagans have moved a lot of the things we associate with Christmas to the Winter Solstice, turning the holiday into their primary winter celebration.

Modern Witches celebrate Yule as the rebirth of the sun (often personified as an infant sun god) and rejoice in the return of the light that begins at the Winter Solstice. For many Witch groups, Yule is also a time of jubilation

> Magically, Yule is a powerful time for new beginnings and for ridding oneself of unwanted habits.

and is celebrated with gift exchanges, toasts for good health, and general merriment. Magically, Yule is a powerful time for new beginnings and for ridding oneself of unwanted habits.

Modern-day followers of Germanic and Scandinavian pagan traditions (generally known as *Heathens* or *Asatru*) have also reclaimed Yule as a Pagan holiday. For many Heathens, Yule has again become a twelve-day celebration beginning on the solstice and lasting until early January. Some Heathens celebrate the first night of this extended Yule period as Mother's Night and dedicate the night to the goddesses they hold most dear. In other groups, it's a celebration of the sun's rebirth or hailed as the return of a sun god or goddess.

More than just a synonym for Christmas, Yule has reclaimed its place at the holiday table as a distinct and valuable religious and spiritual tradition. It's celebrated by Witches, Pagans, and Heathens, and for many secularists and atheists, the Winter Solstice has become a viable alternative to Christmas. (Many major stores now feature "solstice cards" for this very reason.) As more and more people embrace the various traditions of Yuletide, it's likely that celebrations of Yule and the Winter Solstice will only become more prominent.

• EXERCISE 4 •
Host a Solstice Vigil

There are all sorts of ways to celebrate Yule today, from traditional Witch rituals to family gift exchanges around the Yule tree, but one of the most satisfying customs is the solstice vigil. A solstice vigil generally involves staying up all night and welcoming the return of the sun after the year's longest night. It's a time to commemorate the renewal of the light that sustains and powers our world.

Solstice vigils can be solitary affairs or community gatherings, depending on individual circumstances. When engaging in a vigil alone, I often use the quiet and the dark to reflect on the past year, and the power of the rising sun in magical work to help manifest my desires in the coming year. One of my favorite ways to do this is to charge a crystal at sunrise.

There are many ways to charge a crystal with the power of the reborn sun. The easiest is to simply place your crystal in a window facing the east at sunrise and say:

Reborn sun, charge this crystal with your new light. May your energy power me and my work this turn of the Wheel!

For a little extra added oomph, I like to take my crystal outside (weather permitting, of course) and hold it up toward the sun, repeating the same words. Once you are done outside, carry your crystal back inside and place it in your window again to continue to draw in the sun's energy. Afterward, carry it in your pocket or handbag and touch it when you need a magical pick-me-up in the coming year.

Solstice vigils with friends and family can be fun, too. In my extended community, they are often like an open house, with people coming and going. Part of the excitement of the vigil is that you never know who will show up next. They are also great times for gift exchanges or ghost stories or simply for catching up and enjoying one another's company. However you choose to celebrate the solstice, may it be merry and bright!

Christmas

Christmas is the biggest holiday in the Western world in terms of celebrants, popularity, and money spent. It can also be a contentious holiday and is often co-opted by those who seek to wield its power. Over the last fifty years, the phrase "put the Christ back in Christmas" has become popular among Evangelical Christians, but as we've seen, Christmas is far more than just a celebration of the birth of Jesus. And the only real "War on Christmas" in history was waged by Christians who saw the holiday for what it truly was: a mostly pagan and secular celebration.

Certainly, Christmas can be about Jesus if that's what someone desires, but it's not necessary and most of the customs and traditions of the Christmas season don't come from the Christian tradition. Christmas is a holiday with a very tangled-up origin story and is a mixture of secular, ancient pagan, and Christian elements. Holidays are complex things and simply belong to anyone who celebrates them. The fact that Christmas is a secular holiday in the United States is backed up by its status as a national holiday. As the First Amendment to the US Constitution states, "Congress shall make no law respecting an establishment of religion, or prohibiting the free exercise thereof." Christmas is a holiday for everyone and is not reserved only for adherents of a particular faith.

I feel this is worth mentioning, because a book on the Yule season can't help but mention Christmas with regularity. Part of what makes Christmas such a popular holiday is that it has absorbed so many of the customs and traditions that came before it. A book about Yuletide customs and traditions has to include Christmas, even if it has a few edges that some of us are uncomfortable with.

Four Quick Magical Fixes for Yuletide Entertaining

- To bring guests clarity and keep conversations civil, place a few drops of clary sage oil in a spray bottle, fill with distilled water, and liberally spray around your entertaining spaces—before setting out any food, of course!

- Add some sea salt to a decorative holiday bowl, then garnish with a bit of mistletoe or holly and place wherever people gather in your home. Salt is great for soaking up negative energy, and because it resembles snow, will simply look like another Yuletide decoration.

- A few quartz crystals laid out on the dinner table will keep conversations running smoothly, and because they look like icicles, they are inconspicuous.

- If sending out invitations for a holiday party, take a bit of diluted peppermint oil, rub it between your thumb and index finger, then lightly scent each invitation with the oil. Peppermint oil is great for memory and should help people show up on time.

Hanukkah

The celebration of Hanukkah begins on the twenty-fifth day of Kislev and lasts until the second day of Tevet, a period of eight days and nights. Kislev and Tevet are months in the Hebrew calendar, and as that calendar is a lunar one, those dates are variable on the Gregorian calendar (which is the one most of us use). On the Gregorian calendar, Hanukkah can start as early as November 20 or as late as December 26, which means the holiday can last until January 2, though such instances are rare.

Though Hanukkah might be the most familiar Jewish holiday in much of Europe and North America today, it was originally a more minor holiday but grew in popularity due to its overlap with Christmas. Hanukkah celebrates the defeat of the Seleucid Empire by the Hebrew people in 165 BCE, which again established an independent Jewish kingdom. To celebrate their victory, the Jewish people rededicated the great Hebrew Temple in Jerusalem. And though they only had enough oil to burn the lamps in the temple for one day, the light lasted for eight days. This miracle is why Hanukkah is also known as the *Festival of Lights*.

Today, many Hanukkah celebrations resemble those of Christmas and Yule. There's the emphasis on lights, and many families who celebrate the holiday do so with an evergreen tree set up in their living room. Dreidels and menorahs are popular holiday decorations across the world because of their association with Hanukkah. In my own house, we keep an electric menorah on our fireplace mantel to commemorate the struggles and triumphs of the Jewish people, and it has become a cherished holiday keepsake.

Kwanzaa

First observed in 1966, Kwanzaa is a seven-day holiday running from December 26 to January 1 that celebrates African-American culture and tradition. *Kwanzaa* comes from the Swahili phrase *matunda ya kwanza*, which translates as "first fruits of the harvest." Kwanzaa was originally created as an alternative to Christmas, but today the two holidays are often observed simultaneously.

There are seven core principles celebrated at Kwanzaa, with each one being honored on one of the holiday's seven days. The seven principles of Kwanzaa are designed to instill a sense of community among African Americans and celebrants in other countries. The seven principles are known by both their Swahili names and their English translations:

- **UMOJA**: Unity
- **KUJICHAGULIA**: Self-determination
- **UJIMA**: Collective work and responsibility
- **UJAMAA**: Cooperative economics
- **NIA**: Purpose
- **KUUMBA**: Creativity
- **IMANI**: Faith

Kwanzaa has seven core symbols that represent the principles honored throughout the holiday:

- **MAZAO (CROPS)**: These symbolize the work that goes into creating a community harvest. Anything grown from the earth's soil can be used to represent crops.
- **MKEKA (MAT)**: This represents the foundations of the past used to build our lives in the present.
- **MUHINDI (CORN)**: Ears of corn are symbolic of fertility and the family.

- **KINARA (CANDLEHOLDER):** This is representative of ancestry and holds three red candles, three green candles, and one black candle.

- **MISHUMAA SABA (SEVEN CANDLES):** These are symbols of the sun's power and drive away the darkness of winter. The candles are placed in the *kinara*, or candleholder.

- **KIKOMBE CHA UMOJA (UNITY CUP):** The Unity Cup is used to pour out libations to the ancestors and for communal drinking. Drinks are shared to remember those who have gone before and as a sign of family unity.

- **ZAWADI (GIFTS):** These are given on the seventh day of Kwanzaa, with homemade gifts being especially prized.

Kwanzaa is about family and local community and less about decorations and holiday displays. Though there are no official estimates of the number of people who celebrate Kwanzaa, it's thought that thirty million people or more worldwide celebrate the holiday. That's an impressive number for a young holiday, and an important reason why I've included it in this book.

Twelfth Night and Three Kings' Day (Epiphany)

In 567 CE, the Catholic Church began celebrating Christmas as a twelve-day period stretching from Christmas Day to the holiday of Epiphany, or Three Kings' Day, on January 6. Epiphany cele-

Twelfth Night was the lead-up to Epiphany and for many people marked a last night of Yuletide drinking.

brated the arrival of the Three Wise Men to the crib-side of the baby Jesus, and in some parts of the world Epiphany is still the primary day of holiday gift-giving. Never especially popular in the United States, Three Kings' Day is still widely celebrated in many parts of the world, especially Latin America.

Twelfth Night was the lead-up to Epiphany and for many people marked a last night of Yuletide drinking and rowdiness. Twelfth Night was commemorated in William Shakespeare's play of the same name (first performed in 1602), which featured the popular Yuletide pastimes of both cross-dressing and servants acting as noblemen. Traditions such as wassailing were as popular on Twelfth Night in England as they were during the earlier part of the holiday season.

✳ ✳ ✳

Whether you celebrate one or just some of these holidays at Yuletide, it's the sheer number of things going on during the holiday season that makes it special. Yuletide is more than just one holiday; it's an entire season of goodwill and celebration. There are a whole host of holidays in the world today across the religious spectrum, but few seasons capture the popular imagination like Yuletide.

Chapter Two

HOLIDAY FOUNDATIONS

Yuletide is home to a variety of traditions, many of which have been a part of the season for thousands of years. Most of these traditions speak to the very heart of the holiday season: joy, hope, merriment, and generosity. Many of the oldest Yuletide traditions (including Misrule, wassailing, and mummery) have declined in popularity over the last two hundred years, but they're being rediscovered today by individuals in search of older and more authentic holiday traditions removed from mass-market consumerism.

The dominance of Christianity in Europe (and later the Americas) has meant that for the last fifteen hundred years, one of the most identifiable of all Yuletide displays has been the *crèche*, depicting the birth of Jesus. Despite Yuletide being home to a variety of religious beliefs, this impossible-to-escape image has become a part of the season's fabric. Luckily for us, it's also easily adaptable and can be used by nearly anyone for spiritual and magical purposes.

Essential holiday traditions don't have to be thousands of years old, either. One of the most potent and popular expressions of Yuletide mirth and cheer can be found in Charles Dickens's *A Christmas Carol*. The popularity of Victorian-era Christmas scenes is due to some extent to the impact of Dickens's most widely read work. It's also hard to imagine a holiday season without the Ghosts of Christmas Past, Present, and Yet to Come.

Misrule

Since the Roman Saturnalia, celebrations of Yuletide have been marked by what many might refer to as "bad" behavior. December has long been a period of excess and, in Europe and North America, a respite from agricultural work. By December, the harvest has been brought in and the beer, cider, and wine that were produced in the autumn are now ready to drink (and indulge in). In the past, there was an abundance of fresh meat in December, something that just didn't happen at any other time of the year. (Due to December's cold, the meat could be frozen and consumed throughout the winter months.) Combine a full belly, a bit of social jollification through alcohol, and idle time away from work, and you have a recipe for something just a little bit different on the social calendar.

In a sermon in 1712, New England Puritan minister Cotton Mather (1663–1728) said, "Can you in your Conscience think, that our Holy Savior is honoured by Mad Mirth, by long Eating, by hard Drinking, by lewd Gaming, by rude Revelling; by a Mass fit for none but a Saturn, or a Bacchus, or the Night of a Mahometan Ramadam (sic)?" (Bowler, *Christmas in the Crosshairs,* 39). The Christmas in his day had nothing to do with Jesus and everything to do with the excesses afforded by December.

The Christmas described by Mather was not an isolated event, either; the holiday was observed in such a fashion up until the 1800s. Today, many of these behaviors are known as *Misrule,* a custom that was used as a justification for indulgences and behaviors frowned upon by religious institutions. The origins of Misrule date back to the Roman Saturnalia and its penchant for upsetting the social order. The Syrian writer Lucian of Samosata (c. 120–c. 192) wrote that Saturnalia was a time to "let every man be treated equal, slave and freeman, poor and rich" (Forbes, *Christmas*, 8).

With very little work to do, Roman slaves were free to eat good food and consume strong drink, which was often served by their masters. Lucian also wrote that the holiday was a time when "all shall drink of the same wine, and neither stomach trouble nor headache shall give the rich man an excuse for being the only one to drink better quality. All shall have their meat on equal terms" (Forbes, *Christmas*, 9). One of the most popular forms of entertainment at these Saturnalia feasts was the appointment of a Mock King from among the lower and slave classes who could give orders around the house and was expected to encourage less than reputable behavior.

Mock Kings retained their popularity after the rise of Christianity and were a part of many medieval courts. Known by a variety of names, such as the Lord of Misrule, the Bean King, the Abbot of Unreason, and the Prince of Sots (which means "Prince of the Drunks"), Mock Kings were expected to lead Yuletide reveling in a season that often stretched from All Hallows' Eve (better known as Halloween today) through Candlemas (February 2). Mock Kings were also a part of the Catholic Church, with children playfully being elected bishop in honor of the Christmas season.

Lords of Misrule weren't confined to royal courts, either. In Lincolnshire, England, in 1637, a random crowd of revelers elected their own Lord of Misrule, who was promptly "married off" by a fellow celebrant dressed as a minister. Though the couple were in no way married (and it seems unlikely that they were even in a relationship), they did consummate their vows later that evening. Eventually the custom of the Lord of Misrule began to decline in popularity, largely due to the amount of violence that often went into electing one. Lord of Misrule was a coveted position, and one people would fight for.

In some areas of Europe and North America, the custom continued in a less contentious fashion. Instead of people actively campaigning for the honor of being named Lord of Misrule, the appointment was left up to chance. In Belgium, the Netherlands, and Luxembourg, a bean was traditionally baked into a cake, loaf of bread, or pie on Twelfth Night. Whoever ended up with the slice of cake or pie containing the bean was proclaimed the "Bean King" and given a crown and the authority to order around their comrades. Not surprisingly, the Bean King was also expected to encourage heavy drinking.

In other parts of Catholic Europe (and later the United States, especially New Orleans), Twelfth Night guests were served a "King Cake" in honor of the Three Wise Men. The King Cake contained a token baked into it signifying the holiday season, with the finder of the token often expected to take on the role of the Lord of Misrule. In the US, the King Cake tradition is most often associated today with the celebration of Mardi Gras in New Orleans. Since the 1950s, the most common token found inside a New Orleans King Cake has been a small plastic baby figurine. Finders of the baby are often made king or queen for the evening and are generally responsible for buying the King Cake for their friends the following year.

Even as the tradition of electing a Mock King declined in popularity, the high jinks of Misrule were too popular to ever truly go away and could often be found in unexpected places. In the Antebellum South in the US, slave owners continued to practice many of the customs once associated with the Roman Saturnalia. On Christmas Day, slaves were given the day off from work, provided with good food, and encouraged to drink heavily. On some plantations, slave owners even served their slaves on Christmas, and the children of both the slaves and the slave owners were encouraged to play together.

The custom of Misrule spread to other holidays as well. The dreidel has become one of the primary symbols of Hanukkah because it was originally a gambling device. Jews were not permitted to gamble except at Hanukkah. Gambling during the eight days of Hanukkah is most likely an adoption of the medieval Christian attitudes toward the Christmas season and Misrule.

Beginning in the early nineteenth century, the custom of Misrule as a public practice became especially frowned upon, as the holiday season was changed from a celebration of abundance and freedom from work to a holiday about family and children. This was partly due to the Industrial Revolution, since factories didn't have to shut down for the winter, but it was also due to an emerging middle class that actively frowned upon public drunkenness, gambling, and fornication. But Misrule was far too popular to stamp out. Instead, it was transformed for the modern era.

Yuletide office parties are often alcohol-soaked affairs and are seen as a time to engage in behaviors that would normally be frowned upon. Many of the things associated with Misrule have also been moved to New Year's Eve, one of the few days a year when heavy drinking is actually encouraged (and expected) by many parts of the population. New Year's Eve has morphed into the social holiday party that Saturnalia and Christmas once were. It is definitely a night for adults and is not focused on family and children the way many Yuletide celebrations are today. Despite the best efforts of many who dislike the rowdier aspects of the holiday season, Misrule seems destined to continue at Yuletide.

Wassailing

Drinking alcohol has long been a part of Yuletide celebrations, but it takes on another dimension when it is celebrated as *wassailing*. As discussed in chapter 1, wassailing is an old English custom dating back to the Middle Ages and has been practiced in one form or another for over a thousand years.

The word *wassail* was originally a blessing and meant "be of good health" in Old English. The term (and a couple of variants) can be found in epic poems such as *Beowulf* and was originally used as a salutation before drinking. Over the centuries, wassail became synonymous with

TIP 2

Elect Your Own Lord or Lady of Misrule

Electing a Lord or Lady of Misrule to preside over your Yuletide celebrations is always lots of fun. It's a great tradition to utilize when throwing a New Year's Eve party or hosting a Secret Santa gift exchange. There are many ways to randomly select a Lord or Lady of Misrule, but my favorite version involves tarot cards.

First, remove the Fool card from a tarot deck and set it aside. Then let everyone in attendance pick a card from the deck, or, alternatively, simply count out the number of cards matching your number of guests. Instead of including yourself in that number (or picking your own card), insert the Fool card into the deck. Follow this up by having everyone at the party select a card, with the person pulling the Fool becoming the Lord or Lady of Misrule. Be sure to have a crown waiting for them!

drinking, especially drinking at joyous occasions where one might toast to another's good health, such as on Christmas, New Year's Eve, or Twelfth Night. Today, wassail is generally used to indicate an alcoholic drink most commonly made from (apple) cider, though the word is still used when toasting, too!

When people hear the word *wassail* today, they tend to think of it as a tradition closely related to Christmas caroling, which isn't completely wrong. In many parts of England and North America, the working class would visit those more prosperous than themselves and ask for some wassail (or other alcoholic beverage) and/or gifts in exchange for a song, a play, or a drink from a community wassail bowl. (The community drink was generally of a lesser quality than what was expected in return.) Towns and villages with especially conscientious citizens sometimes used the custom of wassailing to collect money for the poor, so that all could take part in a joyous Yule celebration.

• EXERCISE 5 •
Lambswool Drink

Traditional wassail isn't the only drink associated with wassailing. For centuries, *lambswool* was equally popular. Generally made with ale (beer) and whole apples, lambswool gets its name either from its frothy head, which looks like the wool of a lamb, or from the Irish holiday *La Mas Ubhal*, which translates as "day of the apple fruit" and is pronounced "la-ma-sool." Wherever the name comes from, lambswool is a fascinating Yuletide beverage and is a good alternative for people who dislike apple cider.

Ingredients:

- 4 large apples, cored
- ½ cup brown sugar (or more to taste)
- 4 12-ounce bottles/cans of ale (Any type of beer will work, but ale is generally more flavorful. "Heavy" beers such as porters or lagers are examples of ale, in addition to wheat beers and pale ales.)
- 2 teaspoons nutmeg
- 1 teaspoon ground ginger
- 2 cinnamon sticks

Start by coring and then roasting the apples in a 250° Fahrenheit (120° Celsius) oven for about an hour. The apples are done when the fruit becomes soft and mushy and the skin falls away easily from the fruit. Once the apples are finished roasting, set them aside to cool for at least ten minutes.

In a large saucepan or pot over medium heat, add the brown sugar to one bottle of ale and stir until the sugar is dissolved in the beer. Slowly add the rest of the ale and the remaining ingredients, continuing to stir until all the ingredients are mixed together. Reduce the heat on the stove to just below boiling and let simmer for at least ten minutes.

Break open the roasted apples and scoop the fruit out into a bowl, avoiding the skins. Mash the apple pulp in the bowl using either a potato masher or a hand mixer. When you're done mashing them, the apples should be a smooth puree. Using a whisk, add the apple pulp to the ale and spices. Allow the now mixed apples and ale to simmer on the stove for at least thirty minutes.

When you're ready to serve your lambswool, vigorously whisk it to create a froth that resembles the wool of a lamb. The longer you whisk, the more the froth will resemble wool. Serve the lambswool warm using a ladle, being sure to top each cup with froth.

To make nonalcoholic lambswool, substitute nonalcoholic beer or cider for ale. The drink can also be made with wine or hard cider.

✳ ✳ ✳

Meeting the demands of wassailers was an expected part of the social contract up until the middle of the nineteenth century, and the repercussions for not doing so tapped into the destructive aspects of Misrule. Refusal to provide wassail or other gifts often resulted in violence and vandalism, which was one of the reasons the custom began to fall out of favor. Wassail was like an early version of the Christmas bonus, and participating in the custom helped keep the peace between the haves and the have-very-littles.

Though we associate wassail with the Yuletide season today, it was originally celebrated as early as the first harvest in September and often at Halloween. Today's Halloween custom of trick-or-treating is most likely an echo of wassailing. Trick-or-treating, like wassailing, carries with it the promise of mischief for unmet demands, along with the expectation of a small treat.

Wassail was also a tradition that could be practiced in the home. Wassail bowls and cups were common in houses large and small and were filled and passed around at holiday gatherings to family members and guests, accompanied by toasts for continued good health. Wassail bowls could be simple or ornate, depending on the person's level of income (and how much they might like to impress their guests). The bowls were often decorated with ribbons and greenery, especially if they were taken outside the home and used in a community wassailing event.

While wassailing is not nearly as universal in England and North America today as it was two hundred years ago, the tradition has made a strong comeback over the last fifty years. Wassailing is a great way to connect with one's roots and the traditions and history of Yuletides past.

• EXERCISE 6 •

Make Your Own Wassail

There are many different recipes out there for wassail. Because of this, there's no absolute "right" way to make it. About the only ingredient that's really necessary is apple cider of some kind, whether alcoholic or nonalcoholic. I've included two recipes here, the first of which can easily be made nonalcoholic by simply leaving out the whiskey. If you're making a batch of wassail for a Yuletide gathering, I wholeheartedly suggest making at least one small batch of the nonalcoholic variety.

Wassail Recipe #1

- 1 gallon nonalcoholic cider (*not* apple juice—real cider is much thicker!)
- Irish whiskey or spiced rum (I suggest whiskey brands such as Jameson, Red Breast, or Teeling. With whiskey, you get what you pay for!)
- 3 cinnamon sticks
- 1 apple, cored and cut into slices
- 1 orange, peeled and divided
- Cloves to taste (about 10–12)
- A pinch of ground nutmeg (optional)
- 2 slices fresh ginger (optional)

Place all the ingredients in a slow cooker or large pot and allow to warm for several hours. Ideally you want to heat up the wassail to just below the point of boiling, somewhere between 180° and 200° Fahrenheit. (The alcohol in your wassail will evaporate if it boils.) As for how alcoholic your wassail should be, that's a personal choice. I like to add one shot of liquor for every eight

ounces of cider, which means sixteen shots of whiskey/
rum per gallon. (This is less alcohol than in a standard
bar drink.)

For a sweeter wassail, I suggest rum. For a tarter wassail, whiskey is your best choice. And, of course, this recipe can easily be made nonalcoholic by leaving out the
whiskey/rum.

Wassail Recipe #2

This wassail is a bit more traditional since it uses alcoholic
cider. The ideal cider for wassail is "still" cider, which is
easily available in the United Kingdom but difficult to
find in North America, where most alcoholic ciders are
carbonated. For best results, use a "dry" cider, which is a
less sweet version. Try to avoid ciders flavored with berries, unless you want your wassail to taste like a piece of
overly sweet candy.

- 1 six-pack of hard dry cider (12-ounce bottles/cans)
  or 2 one-liter bottles
- 4 tablespoons brown sugar
- Cloves to taste (about 10–12)
- 1 apple, sliced and cored
- 3 cinnamon sticks

- A pinch of nutmeg (optional)
- 2 slices fresh ginger (optional)

Place all the ingredients in a slow cooker or large pot and allow to warm for several hours. You'll want your wassail hot, but keep it from boiling or you will lose all the alcohol in the cider. More or less sugar can be added according to taste, and if you end up using a sweet cider, you may want to leave the sugar out altogether. A nonalcoholic version of this wassail can easily be made by substituting sparkling cider for the hard cider. Another variation is to use perry, the pear equivalent of apple cider.

The Mari Lwyd

One of the most interesting variations of the wassail tradition comes from Wales and is known as the *Mari Lwyd*. Like most wassail traditions, the Mari Lwyd features people out and about in search of drink, but this time they are joined by a skeletal horse—the Mari Lwyd herself! The Mari Lwyd is fashioned out of a horse's skull (or a replica), with piercing glass eyes and often a movable mouth, and is decorated with ribbons and bows. The skull is usually held on a stick, with the person carrying the stick and portraying the Mari Lwyd covered by a blanket or sheet.

While the Mari Lwyd tradition looks quite ancient at first glance, its true origins are unknown. It could be a holdover from mummeries of ages past or a more recent invention. The first recorded instance of the Mari Lwyd dates back only to 1800, but it could be much older. Horse traditions such as the Mari Lwyd can also be found in Ireland and on the Isle of Man, a small island between Northern England and Northern Ireland in the Irish Sea, lending credence to the idea that it might be a pre-Christian tradition.

Mari Lwyd is generally thought to mean "Grey Mare," from the word *llwyd*, which is Welsh for *grey*, and *mari*, from the English *mare*, meaning a female horse. Alternative theories suggest that Mari Lwyd might be a corruption of "Holy (or Blessed) Mary." Welsh folklorist Iorwerth Peate (1901–1982) believed that the Mari Lwyd tradition was related to the Christian Feast of the Donkey (celebrated January 14), which commemorated the Holy Family's flight into Egypt to escape Israel's King Herod.

The traditional retinue for a Mari Lwyd party includes a hostler who leads the horse (and sometimes helps operate her jaw), the combative couple Punch and Judy (traditionally marionettes, but here live actors), and several singers. Traditionally, only men were allowed to play the Mari Lwyd and be among her attendants. Today, Mari Lwyd groups are more inclusive, with women often taking active roles.

Much as with regular wassailing, those engaging in the Mari Lwyd traveled from house to house, offering shows and songs in exchange for food, drink, and warmth. However, in the Mari Lwyd tradition, householders generally put up a degree of resistance before allowing the Mari Lwyd inside. Often this resistance took the form of song, with the Mari Lwyd and her handlers singing a verse asking for admittance and the family on the other side of the door responding in kind. The verses shared between the two sides often featured clever insults from horse to humans and back again. This tradition is known as the *pwnco* and is still practiced in some parts of Wales today.

> Those engaging in the Mari Lwyd traveled from house to house, offering songs in exchange for food and drink.

Once inside, the Mari Lwyd was often a difficult houseguest. She was known to playfully scare children and chase the ladies of the home around, often nipping and biting at them when given the chance. The individuals portraying Punch and Judy were sometimes as fractious as the Mari Lwyd. Punch especially was known to sweep ashes out of the fireplace if not explicitly forbidden from doing so. (Such behavior, though, was generally expected; there are no stories of individuals becoming violent upon a visit from the Mari Lwyd and her friends.) Songs were generally exchanged by the Mari Lwyd and her crew for food and drink, then a blessing was said for the home before heading on to the next house.

Though traditionally associated with Yuletide, the Mari Lwyd can be found in Wales from Halloween to as late as Candlemas/Imbolc. She generally makes her rounds near Christmas or the Winter Solstice but is also a frequent visitor on Twelfth Night. Exact Mari Lwyd customs in Wales differ from village to village, much like the dates of her arrival. Like many of the holiday traditions in the British Isles, the Mari Lwyd all but disappeared at the start of the twentieth century before making a dramatic comeback. You just can't keep a good horse down.

Mummery

Humans have been wearing animal skins and furs for over 100,000 years. For the last 30,000 years, people have dressed up as animals for various reasons. Early hunters wore the hides of the animals they hunted because it allowed them to sneak up on their prey, and most likely for spiritual and religious reasons as well. What better way to understand an animal than to literally be in its skin?

The tradition of people dressing up as animals has a long history at Yuletide and can be found throughout Europe. This practice is most often referred to in English as *mumming* or *mummery*. The word *mumming* likely stems from the old German word *mummer*, which signifies a person in disguise. Many of the customs that are a part of the mumming tradition can be found in both Misrule and wassailing. Individuals dress up and often perform plays or other sorts of entertainment in exchange for food and drink. In addition to dressing up as animals, many mummers went about their business as members of the opposite sex. Cross-dressing was (and is) a large part of the mumming tradition.

Cross-dressing and animal costumes were both popular features of the January Kalends in the old Roman Empire and would later become a part of Yuletide celebrations in the courts and castles of medieval Europe. It was during this period of time that the costuming tradition underwent another change, as many individuals began to simply prefer fancy dress and masks to animal skins or the clothes of their spouse. The Mardi Gras celebrations in New Orleans evolved out of such celebrations and costumes.

In Great Britain, mumming coalesced around the performance of specific plays call *mummers' plays*. What early mummers' plays celebrated has been lost to history, but by the beginning of the nineteenth century, most mummers' plays featured bawdy scripts and at least one humorous sword fight usually starring the Christian Saint George partaking in a battle with a dragon. In most versions of these plays, George loses his fight but is brought back to life with a secret elixir given to him by a doctor. These plays gradually fell out of favor by the start of the early twentieth century, but like many discarded Yuletide traditions, they've made a comeback over the last fifty years.

Mummers' plays were often performed in city streets and in the homes of the well-to-do. The informal staging of such plays led to spectators getting in on the costumed fun and following around the performers. The anonymity offered by a costume often led people to behave badly when out in public—and might be one of the reasons people enjoyed dressing up in the first place!

Mummery is still practiced in parts of Great Britain, Canada, and the United States, with lots of regional variations. The largest gathering of mummers in the world today takes place in Philadelphia, Pennsylvania, where over ten thousand participants take part in a New Year's Day parade that lasts up to nine hours! The first official Philadelphia Mummers Parade was held in 1901, though mummery has a long history in the city.

In Newfoundland, Canada, mumming has evolved into an elaborate guessing game. Mummers (known there as *jannies*) are invited into individual homes, where the house's inhabitants then attempt to guess the identities of the various jannies by asking the masked folks various questions. The mummers don't make it easy, either, often disguising their voices to avoid giving away their identities. The game ends when individual identities are guessed or the guessers give up. This is followed by food and drink.

Mummery is not without some controversy, as the wearing of blackface was common among mummers up until very recently. Most modern mummers decry the practice, but it still shows up occasionally and was part of the tradition for hundreds of years before that. Most

Yuletide customs are welcoming and inclusive; blackface most definitely is not.

Jesus and the Nativity

Visit a department store with aisles of holiday merchandise and you probably won't encounter much that's overly religious. There will be reindeer decorations for the lawn, Santas, fake trees, ornaments, snowpeople, and even light-up dinosaurs holding gifts designed for your front porch (we have one at my house!), but there is one exception: the Nativity scene, or *crèche*. In many households, it's just not the holiday season without a crèche, and it's the same in my home. I have no particular affinity or attachment to Jesus these days, but a small Nativity was important to my grandparents, so it's important to me. Its symbolism can also be interpreted in a number of ways, many of them far removed from Christianity.

The traditional crèche contains the baby Jesus in a manger; his mother, Mary; his human (or adoptive) father, Joseph; shepherds; and the Magi, or Wise Men. The number of Wise Men was not specified in any of the original birth narratives of Jesus, but as the Magi were said to carry three gifts of gold, frankincense, and myrrh, it's traditional to refer to the Three Wise Men. Additional elements of a crèche might include angels and animals (since Jesus was born in a barn, according to at least one account).

There is very little in the Christian Bible about the birth of Jesus, and certainly not a date for his birth. Some Christians have argued that the date of December 25 was determined by estimating the length of his mother Mary's pregnancy, with the assumption that she conceived her child in March. Even if this is truly the case, it doesn't change the fact that most of the trappings we associate with the holiday today came from ancient pagan sources.

The first image of the Nativity dates back to 380 CE, and by the Middle Ages, the crèche was firmly established as a Christmastime decoration. Live-action depictions of the Nativity began in the thirteenth century, led by Saint Francis of Assisi. Today's crèches vary wildly and are a made from a variety of materials. Some of them are extremely traditional-looking, while the one at my house has figures that look like human-tree hybrids rising from the earth.

The stories told about Jesus and his birth come primarily from two sources: the Gospels of Luke and Matthew. Most depictions of the Nativity combine these two stories, as do movies and other media that tell the story

✳

The Cagner

Not included in every crèche but wildly popular in some parts of Europe is the *cagner*. The cagner, or *El Caganer*, comes from Catalonia, a region in Spain, and his name literally means "The Crapper." Traditionally, the cagner is depicted as a Catalan peasant with his backside bare and his "deposit" on the ground. The first known depiction of a cagner dates to the late seventeenth century.

It's thought that the cagner is representative of fertility, and his presence in a Nativity scene is thought to bring good luck. Some believe his poop is meant as a gift for the baby Jesus or is an indication that none shall know the time and place of Jesus's return. The cagner might also just be a joke.

Modern political figures and even the Pope are sometimes depicted as the cagner. Though not a part of most traditional Nativity scenes, the cagner is a fun, if mildly gross, addition to the holidays.

of Jesus's birth, and when joined, they create a far more compelling narrative.

The more "royal" of the two stories is from the Gospel of Matthew. Matthew was writing his story to prove that Jesus was the Messiah of the Jewish people; and at the time, most Jews were expecting an earthly king in the traditional sense, so Matthew obliged. His Jesus is visited by Wise Men bearing gifts, who followed a magical star from the east—just the type of courtly visitors a future king might expect. They also attended to Jesus in a house, not a barn. Traditionally, they visit Jesus on Epiphany (January 6), twelve days after his birth (a period also known as the "Twelve Days of Christmas"), but the writer of Matthew does not specify an exact age for Jesus.

The story of Jesus in the Gospel of Luke was written for Gentiles, or non-Jews. The writer of Luke was trying to prove that Jesus is a deity for anyone who wants to follow him, and not just for the Jewish people. Luke's Jesus story is both miraculous and humble. Angels announce his birth to shepherds watching over their flocks by night, and the newborn Jesus is laid to rest in a manger because there was no room for his family at a traditional inn. The detail of the manger has led many to believe that Jesus was born in a barn, but early tradition places him in a cave that was probably also used to keep animals.

Luke's story was designed to appeal to the poor and downtrodden, while Matthew's story was designed to speak to those with wealth. When the two are combined, they create a story that essentially is for anyone. The stars and the angels add a touch of wonder to the story, too, marking the birth of the baby in the manger as divine. No matter one's thoughts on Christianity, the Nativity tale is a beautiful story. And while it may be many people's "reason for the season," it is only one small part of a much larger tapestry that makes up Yuletide.

As we've seen already, the date of Christmas has very little do with the birth of Jesus and everything to do with the pagan holidays that were celebrated long before Jesus was born. As the twelfth-century Christian writer Scriptor Syrus commented eight hundred years ago:

> It was the custom of the pagans to celebrate on this same day of the 25th of December the birth of the sun. To adorn the solemnity, they had the custom of lighting fires and they even invited Christians to take part in these rites. When, therefore, the Doctors noted that the Christians were won over to this

custom, they decided to celebrate the feast of the true birth on this same day (Bowler, *Christmas in the Crosshairs*, 7).

It is unknown whether the birth of the sun written about by Syrus was being celebrated before the birth of Jesus, but ultimately it doesn't matter. The sun worshippers written about by Syrus celebrated with the same trappings of the Roman Saturnalia and other ancient pagan holidays. And during the era of the Roman Empire, a multitude of groups celebrated the Winter Solstice, many of them doing so days after the solstice itself.

Modern Pagans and Witches often view the Winter Solstice as the rebirth of the sun, with the sun personified as a newborn child. This imagery parallels nicely with that of the crèche, and when I view the Nativity scene set up in my house, I interpret the baby Jesus there as the reborn sun and not the son of God. I see the shepherds and the Wise Men as illustrating that the sun shines down on all of us equally, whether we are rich or poor. I'm sure some of my friends see a Bible scene, but I visualize something different that resonates much more with my own beliefs.

It has become popular over the last two centuries to view the birth of Jesus as a Christianized retelling of far older pagan myths. While it's not true that the story of Jesus is a Christianized version of the myths of Dionysus, Mithra, Horus, and several other deities, it's also not true that Jesus of the Christian Bible was completely unique in religious history. No religion emerges in a vacuum, so it should be expected that Jesus would inherit some characteristics from the deities who came before him.

The humanity of Jesus is stressed by many Christians, but gods such as Herakles and Dionysus also resided among humans in their mythology. The idea of a god that was once seen, touched, and spoken with in the waking world was not unique. In being among his followers physically, Jesus was engaging in a tradition that had begun centuries earlier. Even deities that generally resided on spaces like Mount Olympus were known to visit Earth now and again.

Pagan deities were never born of virgins, but the gods and demigods that resulted from the union of mortal and divine often had miraculous conceptions. Zeus visited the human woman Danae (the mother of the hero Perseus) as a golden rain, which is not far off from Luke's explanation of Mary's conception as "the Holy Spirit will come upon you." The idea of deities fathering mortal children isn't reserved only for mythology; there were many who believed that Alexander the Great was the son of Zeus.

The idea that a human was a god (or could become one) was extremely popular at the time of Jesus's birth. The first Roman Emperor Octavian (63 BCE–14 CE) was hailed as the "Son of God" before he even sat upon Rome's throne. As the adopted son of the deified Julius Caesar, Octavian was viewed as a living god. (Octavian's father was also alleged by some to be the god Apollo.) The idea that Jesus was the son of the Jewish God developed just when Roman emperors were being seen as divine themselves.

Because of Jesus's ties to the deities and ideas of pagan antiquity, I often picture specific pagan gods when looking upon a crèche. Instead of seeing an archetypal sun god, I envision Apollo or Hermes lying in the manger and being honored by those around him. I also sometimes see Dionysus, who was born of a mortal and has always been close to the mortal world. Just because most of society interprets something a certain way doesn't mean we are required to.

At both Yule and the Christian holiday of Easter, a meme comparing Jesus and the Egyptian god Horus often gets shared on social media. This meme lists several parallels between the two deities and at first glance appears rather convincing. But in actuality, the two deities have very little in common. Horus's birth was the result of sexual union between his parents, Isis and Osiris, and no one in ancient Egypt believed that Isis was a virgin.

Most of the material in the Jesus/Horus meme comes from the work of amateur British Egyptologist Gerald Massey (1828–1907). Massey's work has never been held in high regard by scholars, not now or even during his own lifetime. Most every meme equating Jesus with Horus relies on the work of Massey, because Massey is the only source for such things. There are parallels between Jesus and the gods of ancient paganisms, but Horus is not a very good example of that.

• EXERCISE 7 •
Crèche Magic

In many Yuletide rituals, the child born upon Solstice (or Christmas) morning is referred to as the "Child of Hope" or the "Child of Promise." I've always found this to be a powerful turn of phrase, and when looking upon the baby in a crèche, I often envision a world of possibility. The sleeping child can be interpreted as representing a particular deity or a particular goal. When used to represent a goal or an ambition, the crèche can be a powerful conduit for magic.

For this exercise you'll need a crèche of some sort, either store-bought or homemade. A crèche can be traditional (with figures that resemble Jesus and the Three Wise Men) or something more modern. Action figures, toys, and dolls can all be used to create a crèche, with a crystal or stone in the middle to represent the babe in the manger or the goal that you wish to manifest in your life. If what you create doesn't bear much similarity to an actual crèche, don't worry about it. What matters most is that whatever you create resonates with you. (We once created a crèche using figures from the Lord of the Rings movies!)

This piece of magic is designed to be done over a number of days. It might start the moment you set up your crèche or on a date such as December 1. The more days you work on manifesting your magic, the more effective it will be. Working on your intention for a period of weeks is truly ideal. You should plan to finish your work on whatever date is most important to you during Yuletide. This could be the Winter Solstice, New Year's Day, Epiphany, or a day that is personal to you.

As you set up your crèche, reflect for a moment on what the different elements in the crèche represent. The shepherds represent hard work and connection to the natural world and are a reminder that earthly concerns are worth worrying about and fixing. The Three Wise Men are representative of the divine forces in our lives and the joy that comes from giving to others, and they remind us that it pays to be attentive to signs both scientific and miraculous. The "parents" in a crèche can be interpreted in a number of ways. They might be representative of the divine forces (deities, spirits, ancestors, etc.) present in our lives or the love we receive from friends and family. One of the things that makes the crèche such a great place for magic is that it has all of these different elements contained within it.

Once your crèche is set up, write down whatever it is that you are trying to create for yourself this Yuletide season (and/or beyond). Try to be as specific as possible. If you are looking for a new job, include what kind of position you are looking for and what the work environment might be like. Include how much money you are seeking, where the job might be located, and anything else you think might be important. State out loud your intention with your magic, then place your slip of paper directly

chapter two

under the sleeping babe representing the sun and the possibilities before you.

When you are verbalizing your intention to find a new job, it might sound like this:

This Yuletide, I seek a new job, one that will honor my worth as a person and pay me what I am worth. I seek a job close to home that will respect my time and labor. As Yule is a time for rebirth and new beginnings, I place this intention here below the child of promise. My will be done!

Approach your crèche daily, from the date you first stated your intention until the last scheduled day of your magical practice; and once there, write down something you can do to help realize your goal. Using "find a new job" as an example, you might write, "look through job listings online for thirty minutes a day" or "ask friends and colleagues about potential job positions." Looking for a new job is about more than online listings and contacts; it also requires self-confidence and determination. To embody those ideals, you might write affirmations on some days, such as "I am qualified for what I seek and I am a terrific employee" or "I will be successful in my endeavor."

Verbalize everything you write down, ending each statement with "My will be done!" Once you've verbalized your intent, place your written messages under the character or figure in your crèche whose energies resonate most with what you have written. If you've written down "I'm tough, successful, and ready for new opportunities," then you might place that affirmation under the divine parents, if a particular deity or your own parents (or a parent) are responsible for instilling confidence within you. I tend to place physical tasks under the shepherds, petitions for wealth under the Wise Men, and more aspirational things under the divine parents.

You can place your written notes on an altar or other sacred space as a daily reminder of your goal.

After you've written down and verbalized what you can do to help in your magical pursuit, follow up on it. Do the work that you have promised to do. If you've written something more like an affirmation, repeat that affirmation throughout the day, and most importantly, believe it! It does no good to tell yourself that you are strong-willed if you refuse to believe it. Do what you've promised and believe in the words you say!

On the final night of your magic, approach your crèche and repeat your original intention. Then say:

I came here this Yuletide seeking to better my life, and I have put the energy and intentions necessary to do that out into the universe. As we move from winter to spring and the sun grows in the sky, my magic will grow along-side it. With the promise and energy of this crèche and this season, I have worked my will and all will be done as I desire!

You can leave your messages in your crèche until you take it down. Once you've taken down the crèche, go over what you wrote and make sure you did everything you promised to do. You can place your written notes on an altar or other sacred space as a daily reminder of your goal and your responsibilities in achieving it until your desire has manifested. Once you have what you wish in place, dispose of the pieces of paper and thank the universe for helping you achieve your goal.

* * *

A Christmas Carol

Charles Dickens's *A Christmas Carol in Prose: Being a Ghost Story of Christmas* (more commonly known as simply *A Christmas Carol*) is perhaps the most popular holiday story ever written. Since its initial publication in 1843, it has never been out of print and has been adapted for television, movies, radio, and the stage hundreds, if not thousands, of times. It is without a doubt one of the most widely read books of the last two hundred years, and even those who haven't read it are familiar with the story due to its prevalence in our society.

The plot of *A Christmas Carol* is not complicated, but Dickens's story resonates with so many of us because his characters are both memorable and fully fleshed out. There's Ebenezer Scrooge, the miserly boss who is both friendless and destined to be forgotten unless he changes his ways. Bob Cratchit, Scrooge's employee, is downtrodden but also kindhearted, forgiving, and blessed with a large and loving family. The most well-known figure in that family outside of Bob is the sympathetic Tiny Tim, who sees nothing but good in the world despite his disability. Scrooge's former partner, Jacob Marley, makes an appearance as a ghost full of remorse, chained to this world for his misdeeds and ill treatment of others. Perhaps most famous are the three Ghosts of Christmas Past, Present, and Yet to Come, who succeed in turning Scrooge into a kinder, gentler version of himself.

While it's not true that Charles Dickens "invented" the modern celebration of Christmas (despite a recent book and movie making such claims), Dickens did make a tremendous impact on the holiday with his tale. His story helped to popularize the idea of a Christmas spent in the home with family, and it made charitable giving at the holidays not only fashionable but a societal expectation. Think about how many solicitations you receive each year in December urging you to give to charity.

A Christmas Carol has also helped shape the English language in general. *Scrooge* is now a synonym for a cheapskate or one who lacks holiday cheer. It's also sometimes used to indicate great wealth, as in the case of the Scrooge McDuck cartoons by the Walt Disney Company. Scrooge's catchphrase, "Bah, humbug!" is nearly as famous as the character. Today, the phrase is used to signify a curt dismissal of an idea or practice and is popular throughout the year and not only in December.

Dickens also used the phrase "Merry Christmas" in his work, making that specific greeting the most popular salutation directly related to Christmas. Works that used the once common "Happy Christmas" have been retroactively changed to include "Merry Christmas" instead. In the original version of *The Night Before Christmas,* Santa exclaims as he drives out of sight, "Happy Christmas to all, and to all a good night!" But when was the last time anyone heard *that* version of the poem?

One of the things I love best about *A Christmas Carol* is that it's not overly religious. The text includes nothing about the birth of Jesus and creates a Christmas holiday that can be experienced by everyone regardless of their religious beliefs. Bob Cratchit and Tiny Tim do visit a church on Christmas Day, but the rest of the Cratchit family and Scrooge refrain from doing so. The story's most famous line—"God bless us, every one!"—first uttered by Tiny Tim, might sound religious on the surface, but "God bless" is an extremely common turn of phrase. The real power of Tim's utterance comes from just how inclusive it is. He's specifically asking for everyone, regardless of color, creed, or origin, to be blessed at Christmastime.

The Ghosts of Christmas Past, Present, and Yet to Come are both otherworldly and completely magical. The Ghost of Christmas Past resembles both a young child wise beyond their years and a candle. Dickens writes of this spirit:

> But the strangest thing about it was, that from the crown of its head there sprung a bright clear jet of light, by which all this was visible; and which was doubtless the occasion of its using, in its duller moments, a great extinguisher for a cap, which it now held under its arm.

Due to candles and electric lights being so prevalent at Christmastime, it feels as if this particular spirit makes its home in every hearth and home that celebrates a winter holiday.

Dickens controlled every aspect of *A Christmas Carol*, including the illustrations in the first editions. Because of that, we can be sure that the original illustrations produced for the book by John Leech (1817–1864) were just as Dickens intended. Leech's illustration for the Ghost of Christmas Present—with his holly crown, wide smile, well-groomed beard, and cheery, torch-bearing right hand—resembles a modern-day Bacchus, or Dionysus, more than a spirit or an angel, and perfectly captures the contradictions and passion of that particular deity.

In Greek mythology, Dionysus was the god of joy, wine, and abundance, but he was also a god of madness who inflicted punishment on the wicked. The visions shared with Scrooge by the Ghost of Christmas Present represent the best parts of the holiday for many: family, friends, strong drink, and indulgent food. But at the end of the tale, the Ghost reveals that the follies of Want and Ignorance lie just under his robes. The Ghost here is urging us to be aware of the pain felt by others and reminding us that we all have a responsibility to help care for those who have little in our society.

The Ghost of Christmas Yet to Come is the most menacing of Dickens's phantoms. He arrives dressed in a black robe, looking more like the Grim Reaper than a benign spirit. He is silent as he goes about his work, only nodding or pointing in response to Scrooge's questions. The visions he presents to Scrooge are sad and painful, reminding us that our actions have repercussions and that it is our good deeds and not the wealth we accumulate that will determine if we will be remembered beyond the grave.

Dickens is most likely to blame for another holiday tradition, the dream of a "white Christmas." Despite most movies and TV specials painting mid to late December as a snowy winter wonderland, the chances of having a white Christmas in most of the United States are rather small. The odds are even slimmer in London, the setting for Dickens's story, which has experienced fewer than ten white Christmases since 1900. Clearly, the odds are not in our favor when it comes to snow.

Dickens filled *A Christmas Carol* with snowy scenes, a preference that most likely stemmed from his childhood in England during the 1810s. During that period of time, Europe was in the midst of a "mini ice age" that kept temperatures colder than normal. The winters during the 1810s were especially cold and often snowy.

By the time Dickens wrote his most famous holiday tale in 1843, the mini ice age that had gripped Europe was but a memory, but it had a strong effect on him. His Christmas writings portrayed the much colder and snowier Decembers he grew up with, helping to create an expectation that the best Yuletide season is one with snow.

The popularity of Dickens's novella has extended far beyond the original story. Collectible Christmas village sets all tend to look like something out of Victorian England, and many of them feature buildings and places right out of Dickens's story. At Christmas, many large cities now host "Dickens Fairs" (similar to Renaissance festivals), complete with actors as the Three Ghosts of Christmas. *A Christmas Carol* has become an important part of the holiday season, and since it can be easily adapted, it is destined to be a part of things for centuries to come.

• EXERCISE 8 •
Spirits of the Holiday

Whether we realize it or not, most Yuletide celebrations revolve around the idea of holidays past, present, and yet to come. Many of us decorate with heirlooms passed down over the generations. For me, going through the decorations and ornaments we own every year is very much a rich and satisfying journey down holiday lane. Many homes add one or two new wrinkles to their holiday celebrations every year, so no Yuletide celebration is ever just like the one before it. Yule is also one of those holidays that many of us plan for months and weeks in advance; we ask relatives if they are visiting for the holidays long before Halloween.

While we tend to focus on the here and now when it comes to holiday celebrations, the spirits and energies of those we've lost along the way are often near at hand. Both of my grandparents left this world many years ago, but their spirit lives on at Yule in the things they left me and the traditions they inspired. I just can't imagine a Yuletide without one foot planted firmly in the past while my eyes look toward the future. The Spirits of Past, Present, and Yet to Come are the kinds of energies found in most homes at Yule, so why not invite them in?

For this exercise you'll need three taper candles. They can be any color that appeals to you, but I prefer red and green, as those colors are generally associated with the holidays. Once you have candles picked out and put in sturdy candleholders, place them in a prominent place where you celebrate the holidays. For me, this means my fireplace mantel. Place your Candle of Holiday Present in the middle of the space you've selected, with the Candles of Holidays Past and Yet to Come flanking it. This is an exercise I do at the very start of the holidays, when I'm setting up my Yuletide decorations. Since I recommend using long pillar candles here, you might use the same candles several years in a row.

Place something that connects you to past holiday celebrations near your Candle of Holidays Past. This could be a decoration from a deceased relative or a picture of them. It could also be something you made when you were young during the holiday season. Whatever it is, set it by your candle, then light the candle and say the following. If you do this with a partner or the entire family, substitute "We" for "I."

I invoke the Spirit of Holidays Past. May those I've lost remain a part of my Yuletide celebrations, and may the memories I cherish be a part of the magic created in this space. Hail the Spirit of Yuletides Past!

Next, place near your Candle of Holiday Present something you cherish that you received during the past year. This doesn't necessarily have to be Yuletide-related, but it can be. If you've added a new family member, you might place something representing that family member here. When we got our cat Summer, we put one of her favorite toys here for the duration of December. Once you've selected your item, light the candle and welcome in the energies of the present:

I invoke the Spirit of Holiday Present. May this year's celebration of Yuletide be joyful and bright. May all who enter this space create new memories full of happiness and love. Hail the Spirit of Yuletide Present!

Figuring out exactly what we might want in the future can be challenging. When a planned holiday visit from a loved one doesn't quite pan out, I'll sometimes place their picture near the Candle of Yuletides Yet to Come. Another option here is something representing how you see yourself celebrating Yule in the next few years. I want my wife and me to celebrate Yule together both happy and healthy and long into the future, so in years past I've placed tokens of our love near this candle. If you are away from home and hope to return for the holidays soon, placing something representative of home here before you leave is also a great option. When you've selected your token representing the future, light your final candle and say:

I invoke the Spirit of Holidays Yet to Come. May those I love and cherish be a part of my celebrations long into the future. May the Yuletides yet to come be as joyous as those in years past, and may I always be filled with anticipation for the holiday season. Hail the Spirit of Yuletides Yet to Come!

Let your candles burn for however long you can attend to them, making sure to blow them out when you leave the room. For the rest of the holiday season, light them when you are trying to create new Yuletide memories and cherishing those from holidays past. I light them whenever I have company or I'm doing something holiday-related.

Chapter Three
THE GIFT-GIVERS

Gift-giving has been a part of the holiday season since Roman times and possibly even before that, but magical gift-givers are a far more recent phenomenon, being only about eight hundred or so years old. The oldest of those gift-givers is probably Santa Claus, who has become the most popular and well-known Yuletide figure in the world. But there are dozens of other figures who pass out presents to all the good children, along with some who mete out punishment to the naughty. Some of these figures work side by side with Santa Claus, while others were created specifically to replace him.

Saint Nicholas, Sinterklaas, and Santa Claus

The mythology surrounding the figure we call Santa Claus is complex and comes from a variety of sources. The most important origin point is Saint Nicholas, an alleged Catholic saint from the Greek city of Myra (located in present-day Turkey). Nicholas is thought to have lived in the third and fourth centuries, but there isn't much evidence attesting to his existence. His historicity is so dubious that the Catholic Church made the observation of his feast day on December 6 optional in 1969.

During the Middle Ages, most stories about Christian saints emphasized how they had died or whatever judgmental messages they had felt compelled to share. It was different with Nicholas. The tales about him stressed his kindness, generosity, and ability to achieve miracles. He was capable of bringing people back from the dead, and when he died on December 6, it was from old age rather than martyrdom. (Most saints of the Roman period tended to have rather bloody ends.) During the Middle Ages, he became the most popular saint in all of Europe, and with the exception of the Virgin Mary, he had more prayers directed his way than any other once-mortal figure in the Catholic Church.

In twelfth-century France, Christmas celebrations were beginning to become heated, with children going door to door and demanding gifts from their neighbors and threatening people with vandalism and violence if their demands were not met. Hoping to put a stop to such hostilities, a group of French nuns began distributing gifts anonymously to children on Nicholas's Feast Day (December 6). This had the intended effect, and French holiday celebrations calmed down considerably; however, a new expectation of receiving gifts directly from Nicholas in early December had been created.

The custom of Saint Nicholas as gift-giver then spread from France throughout much of Europe. Upon entering the Netherlands, stories of Saint Nicholas at Yuletide became more fanciful. He began riding a magical horse and entering houses through rooftop chimneys. His physical appearance began to change as well; instead of resembling a Greek saint with a short, brown beard, he sprouted a magnificent white beard and stood tall, thin, and regal. These changes were the result of the Saint Nicholas story blending with myths of the Norse god Odin; Saint Nicholas didn't have a magical flying horse, but Odin certainly did! In Dutch, the name of Saint Nicholas is *Sinterklaas,* which is the origin of the name Santa Claus.

The popularity of Saint Nicholas as Yuletide's primary gift-giver would rise and fall during the Christian Reformation of the sixteenth and seventeenth centuries. Catholic areas generally retained their celebrations of Nicholas and observed his feast day with gifts on December 6, while Protestant areas began seeking alternatives and moved the primary gift-giving date to Christmas Day. As tensions between Catholics and Protestants cooled over the centuries, Nicholas generally returned to the areas he had been cast out of. He was too popular to ever truly exile.

The custom of Saint Nicholas as gift-giver then spread from France throughout much of Europe.

Sinterklaas was most likely brought to North America in 1624 when the Dutch founded New Amsterdam, though he didn't make much of an impression in the early days of Colonial America. That would change in the 1800s, and much of Santa's current mythology and appearance is the result of the American influence. One book in particular provided the template for the modern Santa Claus, though it's little known today.

The 1821 book *A Children's Friend, Number III: A New Year's Present, to the Little Ones from Five to Twelve* would have a long and lasting influence on the Santa mythos. Consisting of just eight pages, thirty-two lines of poetry, and eight lithographs, *A New Year's Present* includes most everything we associate with Santa. The gift-giver's name is given as *Santeclaus*, and he pilots a sleigh powered by flying reindeer (though their exact number is not given). Prior to *A New Year's Present,* Saint Nicholas usually traveled on a horse.

In the poem, Santeclaus leaves gifts in stockings and around the hearth. This Santa isn't all fun and games, though. When he visits the homes of bad children, he leaves a "black, birchen rod," with instructions to parents that it should be used when "virtue's path his sons refuse." For an extra fee, hand-painted color versions of the book were available featuring Santeclaus dressed in red and white furs.

Despite the influence of *A New Year's Present*, both its author and its illustrator are unknown. The book's publisher, William Gilley, did not include any credits for the art or the poem in the book, and no one ever bothered to claim credit. Some of Santa's most important creators have been lost to history.

As mentioned in chapter 1, the most influential Santa Claus poem of all time was published in 1823. Generally attributed to Clement Moore, *A Visit from St. Nicholas* (more commonly known as *The Night Before Christmas*) became the standard by which all other versions of Santa would be judged. Moore's Saint Nicholas travels from rooftop to rooftop in a sleigh pulled by eight named reindeer, and instead of being the regal Nicholas of the Dutch, he became "chubby and plump, a right jolly old elf." He's also a powerful magician in Moore's poem, able to fly up chimneys by simply "laying his finger aside of his nose."

It is not an exaggeration to suggest that Moore's poem was instrumental in establishing Christmas as a prominent holiday in the young United States of America. Before Moore's poem, Christmas was a widely known holiday, but its celebration was not universal. (Congress regularly met on Christmas Day until 1855, for example, and the first state to declare Christmas a holiday was Alabama in 1836.) Moore's poem turned Santa into an American institution and, by extension, Christmas into an absolute must in many households. What parent wants to tell their child that Santa will be skipping their house?

• EXERCISE 9 •
Stocking Magic

People have been hanging stockings "by the chimney with care" in Europe since the medieval period. According to a popular legend at the time, none other than Saint Nicholas himself began the tradition when he threw three bags of gold coins into the stockings of a poor family. Nicholas's act of generosity gave the family money for wedding dowries, allowing the three girls who lived there to marry and escape poverty. This story of Nicholas is most certainly apocryphal and didn't begin circulating until centuries after the time of his death, but there's no denying the popularity of the holiday sock.

The question of "why a stocking?" has been asked by historians for the last few hundred years, but aside from the Nicholas story, no one is quite sure why gifts were put into stockings. Perhaps it's because in colder climates, many people would have been routinely hanging their stockings up to dry by the fire, and if that was Nicholas's (and later Santa Claus's) point of entry into the house, then it seems like a reasonable spot to leave a couple of gifts. Whatever the reasons, the stocking is a great place to work a little holiday magic.

Due to its association with presents, treats, and money, the stocking is like a Yuletide cornucopia, or horn of plenty. It's a universal symbol of giving and getting, and when we hang it from our mantels and bookshelves, it becomes a symbol of our wants and desires every holiday season. And on one particular Yuletide morning each year, we get out of bed and find it magically full of gifts and goodies.

We are conditioned from a young age to ask for material things every holiday season, and that can be done with this exercise, but I think our magic has a better chance of being effective when we invite certain energies into our homes and our lives. When I hang my stocking at the beginning of the holiday season, I like to think for a few moments about what's most important to me for the next thirty days or so. Is it being with my family? Staying out of debt? Being a good friend or neighbor during this busy time of year? I then write down that one most important thing and place the note in my stocking (usually just after Thanksgiving) while saying:

Symbol of plenty and Yuletide cheer,
Manifest my desires and dreams here.
May what I care about the most be near,
To be shared with those I hold dear!

After you've placed your note in your stocking, visit your sock at least once a day during the holiday season, focusing on whatever it is you are trying to manifest. Put some of that energy into your stocking each time by verbalizing your wishes or perhaps by letting your own natural energy run through you and into the sock. As a magical vessel for gift-giving, the stocking will amplify the energy you put into it, making that energy more powerful.

On the night before your stocking will be filled up by Santa or a loved one, reach into it and pull out all of the energy that's been collecting within it, and spread it throughout the room. When I do this, I look like a magician pulling a rabbit out of a hat, reaching deep into the stocking and grabbing hold of all the magical energy I can. As you pull the energy up and out of the stocking, be sure to throw that energy around, flinging it to the far corners of your home.

Finally, pull out the original note you left for yourself in the stocking and place it in a spot with personal meaning to you, like on an altar or your Yule tree. As you set the note down, say the following words:

With stocking magic and Yuletide desire,
I now manifest what I set out to acquire!

While Moore's Santa became the accepted version after the publication of his poem, several alternate versions of this figure persisted over the next few decades. Some writers took the "elf" idea a bit too far and made Santa the size of a mouse. Other variants had him riding a broomstick instead of driving a sleigh, and there was even a clean-shaven Santa with a turban on his head. An African-American representation of Santa also existed, forever putting to bed the stupid theory that Santa is only white. Santa was all kinds of things, but the image that resonated the most involved a little old driver who was lively and quick.

Many of the ideas we most associate with Santa Claus came from the Bavarian-born cartoonist Thomas Nast (1840–1902). Nast created the iconic Uncle Sam and forever associated the Republican Party with elephants and the Democrats with donkeys, but today he's remembered most for his contributions to Santa Claus lore. In the magazine *Harper's Weekly,* his Santa Claus was shown as a kindly, plump, older gentleman living at the North Pole. Nast's Santa Claus also dressed in red and white furs and

TIP 4
✳
Santa's Reindeer

"Now, Dasher! Now, Dancer! Now, Prancer and Vixen! On, Comet! On, Cupid! On, Dunder and Blixem!"

Dunder and Blixem?! In the original version of Moore's 1823 poem *The Night Before Christmas*, the names given to two of Santa's reindeer were *Dunder* and *Blixem*, the Dutch words for thunder and lightning. In subsequent edits of the poem, Moore renamed those two reindeer *Donder* and *Blitzen*, the German names for thunder and lightning. Though *Donder* remains the official name of Santa's seventh reindeer, the name is often spelled *Donner* in some versions of the poem.

No one knows exactly what inspired all the names of Moore's reindeer, though it's possible he took inspiration from the names of the god Thor's flying goats, Cracker and Gnasher. Attempts to add more reindeer to Santa's sleigh team have generally been unsuccessful, with the exception of the reindeer with the shiny, red nose.

had a crystal ball that he used to keep tabs on who was naughty or nice.

The image of Santa Claus would continue to be refined in the twentieth century, most notably in the artwork of Haddon Sundblom (1899–1976). Sundblom's images of Santa Claus in a series of print ads for the Coca-Cola Company (beginning in 1931) featured a taller and less rough-around-the-edges gift-giver and soon became the standard for depictions of Saint Nick. Sundblom's images were so popular that they gave rise to the urban myth that Santa Claus's familiar red and white suit was modeled after the colors often used by Coca-Cola!

Starting in the 1980s, speculation began that the Santa Claus myth was directly related to Siberian shamanism. In this telling of Santa's origins, reindeer were his spirit animals and flying in the air on a sleigh was seen as representative of spirit journeying. In addition, Santa's red and white robes were said to come from agaric mushrooms, which share the same color scheme. Sadly, shamans didn't drive sleighs or work with reindeer spirits all that much or ingest much in the way of magic mushrooms, so there's not much truth to this theory, but it is a lot of fun! (Besides, reindeer weren't added to the myth until the nineteenth century.)

• EXERCISE 10 •
Invoking the Spirit of Santa Claus

I have long loved Santa Claus, and I often visualize him as one of the primary spirits of the Yuletide season. His image is inescapable in December and inspires feelings of happiness and joy. When putting up my Yuletide decoration of him (a large Santa doll), I like to set aside a little time just for Santa Claus and invoke his spirit to bless my home with all the magic and wonder of the holidays.

If you've got a prized decoration featuring Santa, that would make an excellent focal point for this exercise. If you don't have a representation of Santa, a printed picture or a red candle would work nicely too. Whatever you work with, set it up in the area of your house that you most associate with Saint Nick, such as a fireplace mantel or wherever the stockings are hung. I also use this invocation of Santa Claus to officially kick off the holidays, and if you've got children, inviting him into your home is a great reminder to kids that he's watching! There's nothing wrong with using Santa to encourage a little good behavior.

Once you've figured out where to put your Santa, hold your Santa decoration (or candle) and approach the area where you will place that item. Envision your happiest holiday moments, whether from Yuletide festivities as an adult or from your childhood. Let those images and feelings wash over you for a moment, then transfer that energy into your representation of Santa. Feel the energy move through your body into your arms and hands and finally into your object representing Mr. Claus. When the Santa object is infused with energy, place it in its designated spot (or light your candle) and say:

I call to Santa Claus, the spirit of the holiday season. Bless this house with love, laughter, and joy, and may it be a space of welcome and comfort for all who enter. Let the energies of peace, kindness, and goodwill be with us this Yuletide, and may we share those energies with others. May the magic and wonder of Yule be present in our rites and celebrations during this year's observance of the Winter Solstice (or Christmas or whatever holiday you choose). Great gift-giver, share these blessings with us this season so that we may share them with those we love.

Harken to us, O Santa Claus, and be with us this Yuletide.
Hail and welcome!

If you're not a big fan of Santa Claus, you can use this invocation with any other gift-giver or holiday spirit; just swap out the Santa name. If your representation of Santa also contains Mrs. Claus, she's easy enough to add in here as well! This invocation also works well in rituals and at the start of holiday parties and can be repeated anytime you need a little extra Yuletide magic.

Tracking Santa Claus

Children around the world today monitor the travels of Santa Claus via NORAD (North American Aerospace Defense Command), a joint military organization established by Canada and the United States to monitor North American airways. On December 24, NORAD provides up-to-the-minute data on where Santa is at any given moment, via the internet, mobile phone apps, and a phone bank staffed by volunteers. "NORAD Tracks Santa" has become a beloved holiday tradition, but it was started completely by accident.

In November of 1955, a child calling to find out the whereabouts of Santa Claus instead reached CONAD

(Continental Air Defense Command) and the phone of CONAD's Colonel Harry Shoup. After a few weeks of reflection, Shoup sensed that tracking Santa would be a public relations win for the organization, so a press release was put together. The following year, the press came looking for CONAD to again monitor the whereabouts of Kris Kringle. The organization complied, and shortly thereafter the program was taken over by NORAD.

As the years went by, NORAD's Santa tracking became more and more sophisticated and interactive. Instead of issuing press releases, the organization released a phone number for children to call. In the internet age, NORAD set up a website allowing children to track Santa in real time, and today there's even a phone app. (I'll admit, I have it on my phone, and it's fun to keep up with!)

Since 2004, the internet search engine Google has offered a similar service. Sadly, Google and NORAD do not work together to monitor Santa's whereabouts, resulting in completely different locations for Santa at any given moment. How confusing this must be for children who believe in Saint Nick!

Christkind

One of the most enduring of all holiday gift-givers is Germany's *Christkind*. Created by Protestant Christian reformer Martin Luther (1483–1546), the Christkind began as an alternative to the Catholic Saint Nicholas. *Christkind* translates from the German as "Christ Child," and Luther envisioned his holiday gift-giver as a toddler Jesus. This figure was often depicted as having blonde hair, a factor that most likely played into the Christkind's evolution.

As the centuries progressed, the Christkind became less and less childlike and more angelic. By the 1700s, the Christkind was most often depicted as a young woman in her early teens, often with wings on her back. The exact reason for this rather radical transformation is a bit of a mystery, but there are some theories. Transporting a bag of gifts for an entire small German village (let alone a country or the whole planet) would have been beyond the physical capacity of a three-year-old, and a taller, older figure was thought by many to make more sense.

Perhaps more importantly, the role of Christkind at holiday markets and other December gatherings was most often played by a young woman. This was due in part to the blonde hair that the Christkind was often portrayed with, but also because teenagers tend to be better actors than four-year-old children. Today, the Christkind is just as likely to be portrayed by an adult as by a teenager, and often resembles a fairy or a cartoon princess, in addition to an angel. Just how the Christkind is represented varies from place to place.

The Christkind became so popular in parts of Germany that she even replaced Saint Nicholas in some Catholic areas! In other places she began teaming up with Saint Nicholas to deliver gifts. She's also responsible for one of Santa Claus's most popular nicknames, *Kris Kringle*. Today, the Christkind is celebrated in Germany, Austria, Switzerland, and the Czech Republic and among the Pennsylvania Dutch in the United States and Canada. The Christkindlmarket in Chicago is perhaps the most well-known American institution with a Christkind presiding over winter celebrations.

The Christkind figure has evolved into a unique part of Yuletide for many, offering a welcome female alternative to Santa Claus. However, in some parts of the world, Martin Luther's original Christ Child is still celebrated as one of the holiday season's primary gift-givers. In much of heavily Catholic Latin America, the baby Jesus is more popular than Santa Claus, and some parts of Europe still celebrate the "Little Jesus" instead of the more angelic Christkind.

La Befana

As magical as Yuletide is, it's no surprise that there's a holiday witch! Hailing from Italy, *La Befana* has been handing out presents to children for centuries. The origins of La Befana are shrouded in mystery, but she has been connected to *Strenia*, the Roman goddess of the new year who was honored during the January Kalends. It's also likely that her name, Befana, is a corruption of *Epiphanea,* the Greek word for Epiphany. Traditionally, La Befana delivered gifts on Epiphany instead of Christmas, though today she's just as likely to share gifts on either day. Traditionally, Befana is depicted as a pleasant old woman riding a broom.

The most popular stories about La Befana tend to involve the baby Jesus and the Three Wise Men. In the most benign of those tales, Befana misses an opportunity to travel to Bethlehem with the Magi and now wanders the earth searching for the baby Jesus, stopping to give gifts to good children on Epiphany and deliver ashes and onions to the bad ones. A more haunting version of the tale features Befana as lost in grief and madness upon the death of her child and suffering under the delusion that Jesus was her son. Upon tracking down the baby Jesus, she presents the Christ Child with gifts, and in return he blesses her as the symbolic mother of all Italian children and heals her mind and spirit.

Another holiday witch haunts Russia with a tale similar to that of Befana. There, the *Babushka* provided faulty directions to the Three Wise Men in their search for the Christ Child. Upon repenting for her sin, she began wandering the world in search of the baby Jesus, stopping to leave gifts on Epiphany for Russia's children to make up for her error. Like Befana, Babushka might possibly be linked to a pagan goddess or other figure from folklore.

Befana is also a New Year's spirit and is seen as symbolizing the transition from the old year to the new. As a broom-riding witch and a pleasant houseguest, she is said to sweep the entrances of the homes she visits. Her sweeping whisks away any bad energies in the house from the previous year, preparing the household for a happy and positive new year.

• EXERCISE 11 •
Befana House Sweeping

There are plenty of gift-giving holiday helpers, but not nearly enough to help with the housework. Celebrating Befana provides a great opportunity to prepare your home for the new year and sweep away anything that's unwanted in your life. For this exercise you'll need a broom or besom. (A broom set aside specifically for magical purposes is sometimes called a *besom*, but any broom will work just fine.) This exercise can be done on New Year's Eve, New Year's Day, or as late as January 6. I usually perform it on the morning of January 1 after cleaning up from the New Year's Eve party the night before.

Start in the back of your home or on the second floor, whichever is farthest away from your front door. Visualize all the "bad" things you'd like to sweep out of your life on the floor in front of you, then begin to sweep. If a room contains negative energy, be sure to clean that up too, along with any negative memories a part of your home might hold for you. As you enter each room, ask for the blessings of Befana with this little rhyme:

Befana, aid me today,
Take all that is negative far away.

Sweep out the old and replace it with the new,
Bring good energies to all that we do.
With the power of my besom and broom,
I free this space from all that is gloom and doom!

Continue to sweep until you've visited every room. When you've gone through the entire house, sweep the negative energy you gathered up toward your front door. When you reach the front door, open it and feel the cold winter air upon your face, then sweep all the bad things outside and away from you. As you send the negative energy outside and away from your home, say:

What's unwanted is gathered here on the floor,
I now send it out and away through my front door.
Befana, help me start this new year off right,
May my home be peaceful, loving, and bright.
So mote it be!

The Yule Goat

One of the downsides to the popularity of Santa Claus is that he often dramatically changes local Yuletide gift-givers. This has been especially true of the Finnish *Joulupukki*, the Yule Goat. Originally a man dressed up in goat skins and resembling a goat, the Yule Goat of today often looks like Santa Claus, complete with a red and white suit. In 1927 a Finnish broadcaster began sharing stories of Joulupukki living on Finland's Mount Ear, a tradition as familiar to Finns as Santa living at the North Pole is to Americans.

One of the most interesting things about the Yule Goat is that he could very well have been inspired by an ancient pagan deity. The chariot of the god Thor was driven by two goats, *Tanngrisnir* and *Tanngnjóstr* (which translate as "Tooth Cracker" and "Tooth Gnasher"), and it's possible that Joulupukki is at least their cousin. Another popular depiction of the Yule Goat is as an assistant to other gift-givers. In postcards, the Yule Goat can be seen walking beside Saint Nicholas and sometimes pulling his sleigh. The Yule Goat as a beast of burden links the figure even more closely to Thor's goats.

Depictions of the Yule Goat made of straw and looking like a goat are especially popular in Norway and Sweden. Most often these straw Yule Goats are placed on the Yule tree as an ornament, but they're also sometimes hidden in the house of a friend or neighbor, who upon discovery of the Yule Goat must then hide it themselves. Due to the variety of ways the Yule Goat is depicted, he will most likely be a part of the holiday season in some way for centuries to come.

Magical Methods to Make Holiday Shopping Easier

Shopping during the holiday season can be a real drag, but you can make it easier with these magical tricks.

When looking for a parking space at a busy mall or crowded shopping center, take a deep breath before entering the parking lot, visualize yourself finding a good spot and then say:

There will be a parking spot for me;
By Yuletide spirits, so shall it be!

After doing this, either you'll find a good spot quickly or someone will prepare to leave their spot at just the right moment.

Shopping can be exhausting, both physically and mentally, especially when the stores are busy. Before heading out to the mall, place a piece of bloodstone in your pocket for extra energy. When you need a boost, take it out of your pocket and hold it in your hand for a minute or two.

The world is full of grumpy shoppers, but don't let their bad energy get you down. Place a small piece of citrine in your pocket while shopping to shield against unwanted energies and keep yourself in the holiday spirit!

Finding just the right gift for some people can be really challenging. To attract just the right present for whomever you're shopping for, attach a picture of your friend or loved one to a magnet and place it in your pocket while you shop. Even better than a picture is a lock of the person's hair! Another option is to simply write down the name of the person you are shopping for on a piece of paper and attach it to the magnet.

No one likes long lines when checking out at a store. To get things moving a little faster, say this spell while waiting either under your breath or loudly in your head:

> *Like flowing water, may this line move,*
> *All blockage in my way I now remove.*
> *A speedy line awaits me,*
> *Checking out is all that I see.*

As you say the spell, visualize everything in front of you moving swiftly and smoothly. (Don't ever envision someone trying to return something or arguing over a coupon!) Repeat this up to three times if it doesn't work immediately. You should be done with shopping and back to your great parking spot in no time!

The Krampus

Over the last several years, the Krampus has become an inescapable holiday figure. Though the Krampus calls Austria and Croatia home, he has become a worldwide holiday phenomenon in the new millennium. Often called the "Christmas Devil," the Krampus is a lecherous and frightening character, and he really does scare children. A friend of mine from Croatia told me that she grew up absolutely terrified of the Krampus and that now, decades later, she still looks at him with fear.

Unlike the other figures in this chapter, the Krampus is not a holiday gift-giver; he's an enforcer. He usually works with Santa Claus and the Christkind, frightening children into good behavior and punishing the wicked. The Krampus is known for spanking bad kids with a switch and tying them up with chains, and when he comes across someone particularly naughty, he throws them in a basket on his back and whisks them away to Hell. The Krampus is not to be trifled with!

In addition to being holiday muscle, the Krampus serves as an assistant to other holiday figures. Sometimes he's Saint Nicholas's driver, and he's been known to carry presents for both Nicholas and the Christkind. He's not always nice, but he does play well with others and wants to see the good children of the world rewarded.

Krampus

The Krampus is also the lecherous spirit of Yuletide. Vintage postcards often depict him as a dapper-looking demon with an especially long tongue, and as a guy who has a way with the ladies. He can be seen in postcards

Elf on the Shelf

Though the two figures look nothing alike, today's popular *Elf on the Shelf* (or *Mensch on a Bench* for Jewish kids) fulfills the same role that the Krampus has for centuries. But instead of punishing the naughty with a chain or a spanking, the Elf on the Shelf runs off and tells Santa Claus about those who misbehave. Like the Krampus, the Elf on the Shelf is a deterrent against bad behavior. (Many of us also think the Elf is far scarier-looking than the Krampus!)

The Elf on the Shelf first came to life in the pages of a book by the same name published in 2005, written by Carol Aebersold and her daughter Chanda Bell and illustrated by Coe Steinwart. This was followed by an entire line of Elf on the Shelf merchandise and even more books. Though Elf on the Shelf claims to be "a Christmas tradition," it's a very recent phenomenon, unlike the Krampus, who has centuries of history.

giving back rubs to hardworking mothers and returning the lustful stares of those mothers. In such situations, he embodied the repressed sexual longing of the Christmas season just looking for some sort of release. Mommy might occasionally get caught kissing Santa Claus, but she was really dreaming about the Krampus.

The Krampus is celebrated in many parts of Europe on Krampus Night (*Krampusnacht* in German), December 5. A visit from the Krampus was originally a prelude to a visit from Saint Nicholas later that evening (Saint Nicholas Day is December 6), though today he's just as likely to visit on Christmas Eve as on his traditional night. Krampus Night was like a "check-in" to see if children really deserved anything from Nicholas. If the Krampus didn't get out his chains and switch or open up his basket, the kids in that household were ensured gifts the next morning.

For centuries individuals have dressed up in Krampus costumes and gone door to door to check up on the children of their neighbors, a custom that is still popular today in some parts of Europe. Krampus parades and runs are also gaining in popularity on both sides of the Atlantic and often feature dozens or even hundreds of people dressed up as the Krampus. No matter where you live today, it's possible to find some sort of Krampus celebration nearby.

The name *Krampus* comes from the German word *krampen*, which translates as "claw." Many people believe that the Krampus is a figure that dates back to pagan antiquity and that he is the son of the Norse goddess Hel, who rules over the dead. He might also be a figure inspired by medieval mummery (which was also an ancient pagan tradition) or a fear of demons. In the early part of the twentieth century, Austrian leaders, along with the Catholic Church, discouraged citizens from celebrating the Krampus but mostly failed. The Krampus was too popular to be consigned to the dustbin of Yuletide memories.

Today, the Krampus serves two roles at Yule. He's around to watch over and frighten children who misbehave, but for adults, he's the life of the party. He should be invoked when you want to shake up your holiday celebrations and embrace the naughtier side of life. The Krampus is the holiday spirit to invite when hosting a wild Yule gathering or when you want to bring a bit of chaos to a prim and proper Christmas dinner with relatives.

• EXERCISE 13 •
A Confident Krampus Chain

One of the easiest ways to tap into the magical energy of the Krampus during the holiday season is to wear a chain necklace infused with a bit of his power. For this exercise you'll need a simple chain necklace, along with any charms you might want to put on it (optional). I suggest a chain necklace made of some sort of metal, in honor of the very real chains Krampus carries with him on Krampus Night.

I've always thought of the Krampus as an extremely confident holiday spirit. One needs confidence if one is going to scold children and show up in someone's home looking a bit like a wild animal. Despite his exotic looks, the Krampus is also a bit of a lothario, which again requires confidence. This exercise utilizes the confident nature of the Krampus to help us feel more secure when dealing with a stressful family, work, or spiritual situation. (I know that I usually don't want to give the toast at the company holiday party, but if I have to, why not ask the Krampus for a bit of help?)

To power up your chain, set it on a holiday decoration that brings you joy or in some sort of sacred space inside your home, like on an altar or even just the top of a dresser if it's decorated with a lot of keepsakes and mementos. When I'm charging mine every year, I like to place it on my Yule tree near one of my Krampus ornaments. Once you've placed your necklace in a spot that works for you, call upon the Krampus and bring his energy into your space:

Krampus, wild spirit of the holiday season, lend your power and energies to my celebrations this Yuletide. Help me to overcome whatever obstacles are placed in front of me and to have confidence in my abilities. May I stand proud and tall no matter the situation, and may my words be blessed with wit and charm. I will be in control of all situations this Yuletide thanks to your power. Hail the Krampus!

Leave the chain in your place of power overnight and visualize the Krampus coming to visit it and putting it around his neck. Wear your Krampus chain every time you are faced with a difficult situation. Be careful not to let the Krampus's confidence overwhelm you, as he often uses it to put himself in amorous situations!

If there are certain things you want the spirit of the Krampus to assist you with over the holidays, you can add some specific charms to your necklace to help. If you are trying to rekindle a bit of romance with a lover or partner, add a small heart or other token expressing love and/or desire to your chain. If you are naturally shy and want the energy of the Krampus to help you overcome such obstacles, add a smiley face or something representative of his horns. I like to recharge my Krampus chain every holiday season and keep it with my holiday ornaments, so I only wear it during Yuletide.

Yuletide Trolls and Elves

Ranging from helpful to mischievous, elves and trolls are regular visitors in many homes during the holiday season. Not surprisingly, stories of Yule elves and trolls are most prevalent in areas that have a long history of such entities. Iceland, Scandinavia, and Denmark are home to some of the most fascinating and frightening of all holiday gift-givers.

Iceland is home to the thirteen Yule Lads (*Jólasveinar* in Icelandic), sons of the ogres Gryla and Leppaludi. Gryla is an especially ancient figure in folklore and is mentioned in the *Prose Edda,* a collection of old Norse mythology first written down in the thirteenth century. In Icelandic Yule folklore, Gryla is a frightening presence whose favorite stew is said to be made from naughty children! Gryla also keeps a black cat who is said to eat any child in Iceland who doesn't receive new clothing on Christmas Eve.

Luckily for the children of Iceland, Gryla's children are a little more forgiving. While the Yule Lads are known for playing tricks on unsuspecting humans, their pranks are usually harmless and consist mostly of slamming doors and stealing certain food items. They certainly aren't looking to eat anyone.

The Yule Lads also have a giving side and are known for leaving gifts in the shoes of Icelandic children in the days leading up to Christmas. Good children are rewarded with small presents and candy, while bad ones generally receive a potato. The Yule Lads make their judgments on who has been naughty and nice daily, so it's possible to get a potato on Tuesday and then treats on a Wednesday.

Often translated as *goblin* in English, the Danish *nisse* and the Swedish *tomte* are ancient nature spirits most often associated today with Yuletide. The nisse and tomte traditionally watch over farms and are said to reward farmers who honor them and punish those who neglect them. Punishment can range from harmless pranks to the killing of livestock, depending on the temperament of the individual nisse or tomte.

Most nisse and tomte today appear around Yuletide and often deliver gifts door to door to children on Christmas Eve. Traditionally these holiday figures were short, about three feet tall, but now they are often depicted in a manner similar to Santa Claus. The nisse and tomte are usually rewarded for their generosity with a bowl of warm porridge topped with butter. Failure to leave them an offering sometimes results in the nisse or tomte playing pranks on those who have overlooked them.

Unlike gift-givers such as the Christkind or even the Yule Lads, there are many tomte and nisse, and not all children are visited by the same figure. This links both figures to the pre-Christian past of Scandinavia, when both types of spirits were either related to a form of ancestor worship or seen as members of the fey, or creatures from the land of fairy. The tomte are enjoying somewhat of a revival right now, and ornaments and figures honoring them can be found in many department stores, where they generally resemble garden gnomes.

• EXERCISE 14 •

Honoring the Fairy Folk of Yuletide

The fairy folk are humanlike entities that we share this world with. They are most often found living outdoors in natural settings, but not exclusively so. Up until the seventeenth century (and long past that in some places), the fairy folk (also known as the *fey* or *fair folk*) were generally considered fearsome by most human beings. Even today, many who are close to the fair folk advise caution when interacting with them. The fey are not energies to be bossed around, but rather sovereign beings with their own free will.

Though the fairy folk typically live outside, there are some who enjoy the warmth of a cozy home and the company of human beings. If they are shown deference and honor, the fey make fabulous houseguests. If they feel as though they are being mistreated, you might find yourself unable to find your car keys in a timely manner or the milk in your fridge expiring earlier than you'd like. Due to the magic and twinkling lights in most homes at Yuletide, you may end up with a member of the fair folk staying with you over the holidays.

Once a member of the fair folk has been invited into someone's home, they will usually stay there indefinitely,

chapter three

and once they are given offerings, they will expect them going forward. If you suspect that a member of the fair folk is visiting you this Yule, welcome them inside for the season so they know the invitation is not open-ended. Also, be prepared to leave them offerings for the duration of their stay.

Any food or drink item can be left for the fey as an offering, but it's best when that item is something you value. Giving them the wine you don't want to drink is not an offering; it's an insult. So be prepared to give them at least whatever you are eating and drinking. In my experience, the fey enjoy alcohol, good food, and cream. The fey do not eat or drink as we do, but rather consume the essence of a thing, meaning that the offering's physical substance will still be present after it is consumed. Twenty-four hours after presenting the fey with an offering, it is customary to dispose of the offering either in the garbage, outdoors, in the compost bin, or in a fire. (It's considered bad manners to eat the remains of an offering.)

For this exercise you'll need a small bowl or dish and a spot in your home that no one is likely to disturb. Giving

> The fey do not eat or drink as we do, but rather consume the essence of a thing.

the fey a piece of cake as an offering only to have your spouse turn around and eat it will result in some angry fairy folk! When you've picked out your dish and quiet spot, address the fey so they will know that you've prepared a place for them and how long their stay is expected to last. I usually say something like this:

This Yuletide, I happily greet the fair folk who have come into our home! Blessed guests, be a part of our magic and merrymaking this Yule. Join us in our celebrations as honored visitors. Find sustenance and honor here from today forward through Twelfth Night as we share this Yuletide together. Be welcome and partake of our good cheer!

Once you have presented the fey with an offering, it's best to refresh that offering at least once every forty-eight hours. When leaving a new offering, be sure to address the fair folk once more to let them know that what you've left out is specifically for them. This does not have to be elaborate; a simple "to the fey!" will work. If you celebrate a particular Yuletide holiday with extra fervor, perhaps the Winter Solstice or Christmas, leave them a little extra that day to make them feel a bit more like a member of the family.

TIP 6

That's a Wrap

Instead of buying new wrapping paper every year, reuse the paper that's already in your house. This can be more than just last year's wrapping paper; newspapers, magazines, maps, and posters all make attractive gift wrap. Place a reusable cloth bow around your gift and you're ready to go!

Don't forget that most gift bags can be used more than once or twice, too. As long as a bag still looks presentable, keep on sharing! This goes for boxes as well. My family has been wrapping the same boxes and putting them under the tree for over twenty years now.

Chapter Four
HOLIDAY TRADITIONS

Yuletide is home to an abundance of holiday traditions and customs from around the world. Many of these traditions date back to pagan antiquity, while others are far more recent in origin, and a few are a combination of both. No matter their origins, items such as mistletoe, evergreen trees, and poinsettias have become a vital and magical part of the Yuletide experience. For many of us, it just wouldn't be Yule without a nutcracker on the mantel or a Yule log in the fireplace.

The Christmas Tree

Evergreen trees and branches have long been associated with December holidays. The Romans decorated their homes with evergreen branches and wreaths during Saturnalia, which dates much of the custom to ancient pagandom. A first-century Roman mosaic from Tunisia in North Africa features a joyous Dionysus entering the town with a full-grown (though rather scanty) evergreen tree. This image has been used as evidence to suggest that the Romans might also have celebrated the Saturnalia season with a full-grown tree instead of simple branches. Though it's certainly possible, no other evidence has emerged to support the idea.

What's probably most important is that evergreen boughs were quickly adopted by Christians as a way to decorate for Christmas. When exactly the entire tree began to be used for holiday celebrations is a mystery. Many historians give the Christian reformer Martin Luther credit for decorating the first Christmas tree. Luther's tree would have been much like the ones many of us have in our homes today, though far more dangerous, as early Christmas trees were often decorated with lit candles. Talk about a fire hazard!

The Christmas tree, or at least something very similar to it, most likely predates Luther, though. Medieval mystery plays featuring stories from the Christian Bible often featured a *paradise tree*, which was typically an evergreen tree of some sort decorated with apples and communion wafers. The most popular mystery play near Christmas was the tale of Adam and Eve (who, according to Hebrew legend, were the world's first man and woman), which was enacted on December 24, the Catholic feast day of Adam and Eve. The story of Adam and Eve is familiar to most of us and includes a serpent tempting Eve to eat the fruit of the "tree of the knowledge of good and evil," despite her god telling her the fruit was off limits.

The evergreen typically represented the tree, and the apple the forbidden fruit. The play then generally ended on a downer, with Eve and Adam being exiled from paradise. With the paradise tree already set up in churches and the castles of medieval nobility, it's not hard to imagine the tree being turned into a symbol of Christmas the following morning.

An older, and still Christian, explanation for the Christmas tree also comes from Germany and involves the eighth-century Saint Boniface, who did the majority of his missionary work in Germany, despite being born in

England. In this tale, on Christmas Eve Boniface races to a pagan German village where a small child is due to be sacrificed to the god Thor near a large oak tree dedicated to the deity called the *Thunder Oak*.

The Thunder Oak was apparently quite large, but Boniface was said to have chopped it down with just one or two strokes of his ax. After the tree fell to the ground, Boniface pointed to a small evergreen tree near the old Thunder Tree and proceeded to tell the astounded pagans that the evergreen represented the immortal life promised by Jesus. This story is most certainly not true, but it might be representative of some actual pagan beliefs. There were many German pagans who believed that trees harbored spirits within them, so decorating with an evergreen tree would have been a way to bring those spirits into a home.

The story of Boniface has also led some people to believe that the ancient Celtic Druids had something to do with the invention of the Christmas tree. In some versions of Boniface's story, the people honoring the Thunder Oak were said to be Druids, thereby linking the Druids to the Christmas tree. But Druids wouldn't have been in Germany in the eighth century, though in some medieval stories anyone who practiced a pagan faith or was a magic user was said to be a "Druid."

Yet another origin for the Christmas tree might come from the German tradition of the Christmas pyramid, or *lichstock*. Despite the name, a Christmas pyramid does not actually resemble a pyramid. In medieval times, the pyramids were four-to eight-sided platforms containing evergreen branches, fruit, biblical scenes, and gifts, with candles on top, and were traditionally hung from the ceiling. Originally they were used at a variety of holidays, such as Midsummer (the Summer Solstice), but eventually they became associated only with Christmas.

Christmas pyramids are still popular in Germany and other parts of Europe, but they don't look much like the medieval versions that inspired them. Today, Christmas pyramids resemble a carousel with several different levels and are most often decorated with scenes from the Nativity. They also show up in giant form in many parts of Europe, where they are popular attractions in parades and at Christmas markets.

After their adoption or invention by Martin Luther, Christmas trees became very popular in Germany, but it would be a few centuries before they were brought to the

TIP 7

✳

Christmas Tree Lights

The earliest Christmas tree lights were candles, which up until the twentieth century were surprisingly expensive. Families that could afford candles for their trees generally only lit them for a few minutes before blowing them out.

The first set of electric Christmas tree lights was created in 1882, but electric lights didn't really catch on until the 1920s, when mass production and the assembly line made them affordable. Though safer than candles, early electric lights were still dangerous, as they were often incredibly hot.

Today's electric tree lights are better than ever and safer too. LED lights, which are cooler to the touch, have significantly lowered the risk of fire and are far more durable. A good set of LED lights should last for years, which beats having to go through your lights every year to replace burnt-out bulbs.

English-speaking world. (People did, however, still decorate with evergreen branches during this period in the United Kingdom and the United States. They just didn't use whole trees.) As mentioned in chapter 1, Christmas trees first became popular in England due to the influence of Prince Albert, the husband of Queen Elizabeth. After his marriage to Elizabeth in 1840, Albert began decorating the royal residence with the German Christmas tree, inspiring millions of others to begin the tradition in England and later in the United States.

For many families, the holidays revolve around artificial Christmas trees. The first artificial trees were built in nineteenth-century Germany and were made out of feathers! These trees were most often made out of dyed-green goose feathers that were wrapped around wire "branches" attached to a wooden dowel. Feather trees were extremely popular in Germany at the turn of the twentieth century and were later imported into the United States. These trees were pretty, but the feathers were not strong enough to support ornaments, limiting their popularity.

For a few short years in the US in the late 1950s and early 1960s, the most common artificial tree was the aluminum Christmas tree, made from aluminum, of course.

Looking like something out of *The Jetsons*, aluminum trees were perfect for the Space Age and were just as likely to be red, silver, or gold as green. Many of them came with a spinning color wheel that projected a rainbow of different colors on the tree. The aluminum tree craze lasted less than ten years but was immortalized in 1965's *A Charlie Brown Christmas*.

By the 1980s, most artificial trees were being made out of PVC plastic, which is still the case today. PVC plastic is an extremely versatile material and makes for a very realistic-looking Christmas tree. Even better, plastic branches made from PVC are strong enough to hold even the heaviest ornaments.

No matter what kind of holiday tree you choose (real or artificial), you can make your choice environmentally green. If you decorate with a real tree at Yule, buy one from a local Christmas tree farm instead of the grocery store. The carbon footprint of a local tree will be substantially less than that of a tree shipped from hundreds of miles away. Trees are also great carbon collectors, which helps in the fight against global warming and climate change.

When you're through with your tree in early January, resist the urge to throw it in the garbage. Most cities collect trees after the holidays and turn them into useful mulch. If you've got room to spare in your backyard, buy a live tree (yup, with roots and all!), then plant it after the holidays or when the earth thaws in the spring. Don't want to bother planting a tree? There are many companies that now rent holiday trees, offering free delivery and pickup.

If you're looking for a new-to-you Christmas tree, be sure to visit your local secondhand stores and check the online classified ads. Buying a used artificial tree is good for the planet and keeps a serviceable tree in use and out of the local landfill. Even the ugliest artificial tree will look good with a bit of garland and a few strings of lights!

Christmas trees feel timeless today, but a great majority of the world didn't utilize them until the nineteenth or twentieth century. Even if the decorated tree is a relatively new custom, it still connects us to our ancestors and to the natural world. Evergreen trees were chosen as Christmas trees for a reason: they are a reminder that life continues even in the cold dark of winter. That was true for the Romans and it's true for us as well.

• EXERCISE 15 •

Magical Ornaments

Christmas trees are one of the most magical items in any household during Yuletide. The ornaments on a Christmas tree often serve as sneak peeks into family histories. The branches of most Christmas trees likely hold decorative treasures from long-ago Yule celebrations or keepsakes from vacations and other life events. The simple act of picking out a tree at a Christmas tree lot or farm also serves as a bonding experience for many. I will never forget trudging through the snow with my father and brother for two hours searching for just the right tree. We did eventually find it—in the Christmas tree farm's selection of precut trees.

But perhaps most importantly, Christmas trees are liminal spaces, and liminal spaces are truly magical. Many Witches work their magic in spaces that are said to "exist between the worlds," and many cultures view the crossroads where two paths meet as magical spots. Christmas trees are liminal because they are where many of us give and receive presents. In the days leading up to Yule, I place gifts for my family under the tree, and on the morning of the gift-giving, the tree becomes the place where I receive them. The Christmas tree, then, is a site for giving and receiving.

This makes the Christmas tree an especially powerful magical partner, because the tree and the area around it are infused with those energies. We can put those energies to work for us in powerful ways that are also fun and decorative! Creating ornaments for the tree is one of my favorite kinds of Yuletide magic, and it can be done to help satisfy a whole host of wants and needs.

For This Exercise You Will Need:

- Clear, fillable plastic ornaments (These are easily found online in most craft and hobby stores and are also very inexpensive.)
- Hooks for your ornaments (if they are not already included with your ornaments)
- Items to put in your ornaments

For those of you with extra artistic skill, an alternative to a fillable ornament is a clear glass ornament. Instead of filling glass ornaments, you can paint them, utilizing colors and symbols that represent the forces you are trying to bring into your own life or someone else's. Oftentimes glass ornaments turn out looking better, though I think they lack a bit of the magical punch that fillable ornaments containing herbs and stones have.

Just what you'll need to add to your ornaments depends on what it is you are trying to accomplish. Anything can be added to these types of ornaments, but ideally you'll want to add items that not only look nice but also serve the magical purpose of the ornament. Herbs are great for ornaments, but make sure that anything that is likely to rot is dried out before you add it, or make plans to remove the potentially problematic item when you take down the Yule decorations. Here are some items to add to your ornaments listed by category.

HAPPINESS: Picture of a smiley face, peace sign, amethyst, lapis lazuli, hematite, poinsettia leaves, ivy, holly, images/pictures of places, people, or pets you love

HEALTH: Rod of Asclepius, picture of the sun or moon, yin-yang symbol, citrine, dried lavender, dried ginger, oak leaves

LOVE: Cinnamon stick, heart, cherub (Cupid) picture, seashell, dried rose petals, magnet, rose quartz, moonstone, mistletoe

WEALTH: Coins (chocolate Hanukkah coins wrapped in gold foil are great!), paper money, dollar signs, a small wrapped gift box, holiday paper, gold, picture of the Three Wise Men (they were also kings, you know!) emerald, fuchsite, garnet, a holiday

gift-giver, High John the Conqueror root, anything green (such as a bit of an evergreen tree)

As you place your items in the ornament, think about
what you are trying to accomplish with your magic. If
you're making a wealth ornament, visualize yourself content at work and financially secure. Picture yourself giving and receiving love, if that is something you are looking to bring more of into your life. For me, happiness
and freedom from stress during the holiday season is a big
request. The presents, decorating, and social obligations
can all be a bit overwhelming, so visualizing myself happy
and content is especially appealing.

Ideally you'll want to fill your ornament in a way that's
visually appealing. This can be more challenging than it
sounds but can be accomplished with some patience and
some superglue. For a love ornament, I once glued three
rose petals directly onto the inside of the ornament and
placed a cute picture of Cupid toward the back of
the globe (where it would stand up straight on its
own), then added a reasonably sized seashell
in front of Cupid. Next I added some red
and pink ribbon to the ornament to give it
a little extra sparkle. Super easy! Ribbon,

bows, and tinsel are all easy add-ons to fill up your ornament. Just pick a color that matches your theme.

Once you've filled up your ornament, close it up and then hold it in your hands and think about its purpose. Imagine walking by it during the holiday season and reflecting on the meaning behind it. Now approach your tree and place your ornament in a spot that will be easy for you to see on a daily basis. If you're using the ornament as a way to give something to others, such as good health, a job, or wealth, say the following:

I place this ornament in the magical space of my holiday tree. Here, around this tree, the power of generosity and goodwill toward others gathers to be shared by all who would reap its rewards. May this ornament bring about the favor I ask of it this holiday season!

If the purpose of your ornament is to receive something for yourself, say the following words:

In the branches of my holiday tree, I place this ornament. May it bring into my life the things I wish to see manifest. By the power of the Yuletide and the magic of the holiday season, may this ornament bring about the change I seek in my life!

Over the next few weeks, reflect on the meaning behind your ornament every time you walk past it. This doesn't have to be a long period of reflection, but pause long enough that you can clearly visualize what it is you are trying to bring into your life or someone else's. If what you are seeking does not come to pass completely during the Yuletide, the ornament can be placed in a space that is special or sacred to you. If it did work, thank its energies for assisting you and pack it up with your other ornaments at the end of the season. To reactivate the ornament the following year, simply say the previous words again and visualize what it is you are trying to accomplish.

If negativity or the ill will of others threatens your holiday season, there is another magical technique that utilizes empty ornaments. For this one, all you'll need is some gold or silver tinsel/garland, some dimes, anything else that's shiny or reflective, and possibly a small mirror, if desired. The idea here is that your ornament will reflect all the negative energy directed at you and your family during the holidays back to its point of origin. The best part of this is that these ornaments also look great because of the tinsel!

After you've filled up your ornament, walk up to your tree and visualize everyone you care about feeling happy and content during the holiday season (especially if they will be in your home in December/January). Picture any negative thoughts being directed your way bouncing back to the sender. With that picture clearly in your mind, place the ornament on the tree while saying:

May our holiday space be safe and protected from all who would wish to disrupt our happiness. All that is unwanted will be reflected back and away from those who celebrate here. Let our Yuletide be merry and bright and free of strife!

At the end of the holidays, the ornament can be packed away with the others and reactivated the following year.

• EXERCISE 16 •
Tarot Ornaments

Over the years I've collected a lot of tarot decks and, somehow, a lot of loose tarot cards. An easy way to decorate your holiday tree is with those extra cards! Tarot cards make great ornaments because they have specific meanings to many of us, and the art on them is colorful and often highly reflective. Beloved tarot images reflecting red, green, or blue light are highly pleasing!

Turning a tarot card into an ornament is simple and requires only a hole punch and a piece of string or a paper clip. It's natural to assume that the hole should be made directly in the middle of the top of the card, but the sides work too, especially if the hole might mar the image. One of the great things about ornaments is that they don't have to hang exactly straight.

For those who really love tarot, an entire tree decked out with a complete set of cards is a sight to see! For those just starting out who don't have much in the way of ornaments, a thirty-dollar deck of cards can take care of all your tree-decorating needs. For those who like to top their tree with a star, most decks even come with a Star card.

The Yule Log

The Yule log of today takes several different forms. For some, it remains what it's been in ages past: the primary piece of wood in a cheery Yuletide fire. At my house, our Yule log is decorative: a slab of wood adorned with holiday decorations, with spaces drilled into it for some tealight candles. Many folks honor the Yule log as the *bûche de Noël*, an edible treat decorated to resemble a piece of wood. Services like Netflix offer our televisions and computer screens "streaming Yule logs," providing the warm glow of a fire without needing a fireplace. Because of these various permutations, the Yule log is probably far more popular today than ever before, but few people realize just how important it once was at Yuletide.

For centuries the Yule log was one of *the* centerpieces of Christmas and Yule celebrations. The first recorded reference to the Yule log dates all the way back to 1184 in Germany, and given that date, it's likely that the Yule log as a custom is far older than that, and probably predates the adoption of Christianity in Germany. From Germany, the custom of the Yule log spread throughout Europe and was firmly established in England by the early 1600s, when it first showed up in the written record. Shortly thereafter, the custom reached North America, and it's been a part of Western holiday traditions ever since.

Yule log traditions vary across Europe and the Americas, but for centuries finding a suitable Yule log was an extremely important activity. In England, the Christmas Day Yule log was selected on the holiday of Candlemas (February 2) and then set out to dry until its use eleven months later! In other parts of Europe, families would wake up with the sun and seek a Yule log in the early morning hours on Christmas Eve. In Norway, it was customary for the male head of the household to find the Yule log on his own.

Simply dragging the Yule log home was a cause for celebration in many places. Yule logs were decorated with ribbons as they were dragged home in the snow or mud, and small children were sometimes permitted to ride on top of the Yule log as others labored. Those not intimately involved in the transport of the Yule log often cheered on those who were, making the entire exercise festive.

Once inside the home, the Yule log often had to be ceremonially placed on the fire. Often that meant dousing the log with wine or grain for health and prosperity in the coming new year while a prayer or blessing was spoken. In Newfoundland, Canada, once the log was set in the hearth, it was customary to celebrate by shooting a gun outside as a way of sharing Yule log success with the neighbors. On certain American plantations in the pre–Civil War South, slaves were free from work for as long as the Yule log burned. For this reason, the log was often heavily sprinkled with water so it would burn longer.

In many households, it was customary to kindle that year's Yule log with the ashes or remnants of the previous year's log. But the ashes of the Yule log were important for a variety of magical reasons as well. In some areas, they were used to cure diseases in cattle, prevent mildew on crops, fertilize soil, and relieve toothache pain. Ashes thrown into a hearth were believed to drive off life-threatening storms and protect against bad weather.

In Germany, the *Christbrand* was a piece of wood similar to the Yule log, but instead of being allowed to burn completely, it was taken out of the fire once it was lightly charred. This piece of wood was kept around the rest of the year and thrown into the fire anytime bad weather threatened. In Scotland, the *Cailleach Nollaich* (or Christmas Old Wife) was a tree stump or large root carved to resemble the head of an old woman. The carved root/stump was symbolic of evil and thrown into the household fire on Christmas Eve, where it was allowed to burn down completely. It was believed that burning the Cailleach Nollaich would keep negativity and harm away for the coming year.

For many homes without a fireplace, the Yule log has become a fixture on television and computer screens. The first television broadcast of a burning Yule log took place in

TIP 8

*

The Magic of Wood

Any kind of wood is appropriate for a Yule log, but burning particular types of wood can infuse your home with certain energies. The following are some of the more common woods used for Yule logs, along with some of their magical properties:

Apple: Abundance, love, healing
Ash: Prosperity, protection, health
Birch: Protection, purification
Cherry: Divination, prosperity, sweetness
Fir: Rebirth, long life, health
Oak: Fertility, health, stability, healing, luck
Pine: Resilience, healing, money

1966 on WPIX, a television station out of New York City. It was broadcast in black and white and utilized a seventeen-second loop shot in the residence of New York City's mayor. Like most Yule log broadcasts today, it was accompanied by holiday tunes and aired for several hours. It originally aired on Christmas Eve and early Christmas morning.

Over the ensuing decades, the tradition of the broadcast Yule log spread from coast to coast and into Europe. Today's virtual Yule logs are in full color and can be found in a variety of outlets, from streaming services to traditional broadcast outlets. Several feature references to fictional characters or show Santa with his feet propped up! In addition, there are many alternatives to the virtual Yule log available online, including a video featuring Darth Vader's funeral pyre and a raging dumpster fire.

• EXERCISE 17 •
Chocolate Peanut Butter Bûche de Noël

One of the most popular kinds of Yule logs doesn't go in the fire; it goes into our bellies. Invented in France during the nineteenth century, the *bûche de Noël* (literally "Christmas log") has become a worldwide holiday treat. Designed to resemble a traditional Yule log, the bûche de Noël is a rather complicated piece of baking but is well worth the extra trouble and hassle. Today the treat is associated most with Christmas but is popular in France throughout December and up until Epiphany. In other words, the Yule log is not just for Christmas or even Yule.

There are several different ways to make a Christmas log, but traditionally the treat is a rolled-up sponge cake with a filling of some sort and a generous amount of buttercream frosting on the outside. Often all of the parts of the log are made from scratch, but as I'm not much of a baker, I've chosen to go a different route. This Christmas log recipe features a homemade sponge cake (there's no way around this part), with a filling of store-bought peanut butter and topped with chocolate frosting from the baking aisle. For those who want to do all the heavy lifting, there are many great recipes online for homemade filling and frosting.

For those interested in doing a little extra decorating of their Christmas log, I've included a recipe for marzipan at the end of this exercise. Marzipan is an edible dough that can be shaped into all sorts of wonderful things. Traditionally, Christmas logs include decorative mushrooms and flowers, which are super easy to make with marzipan. Adding such flourishes is entirely optional, but if you've got a free half hour, it can be a lot of fun. It's also something that can be done as a family activity.

Ingredients:

- Nonstick cooking spray
- ¼ cup unsweetened cocoa powder
- ½ cup all-purpose flour
- A generous pinch of salt
- 7 eggs, separated
- ¾ cup regular white sugar, halved
- Powdered sugar, enough to sprinkle on a towel
- A jar of your favorite peanut butter (Don't like peanut butter? There are alternatives, including jellies and jams, Nutella, or more frosting!)
- A jar of chocolate frosting (traditionally buttercream)
- A small bar of white chocolate

You Will Also Need:

- A jellyroll cake pan (a baking sheet with a one-inch lip, generally about 10½ by 15½ inches)
- Parchment paper
- 3 bowls for mixing, two large and one smaller
- Spatula

- A clean towel
- Cheese grater

Directions:

Preheat the oven to 350° Fahrenheit and spray the jelly-roll pan with cooking spray. Line the pan with parchment paper and generously spray the paper with more cooking spray.

Mix the cocoa powder, flour, and salt in a small bowl. Set aside.

In a large bowl, beat the egg yolks until they thicken. If using a fork, this will probably take at least five minutes. Slowly add in half of the white sugar, continuing to beat the yolks along with the sugar. Once those two ingredients have been mixed together, slowly introduce the flour/cocoa powder/salt mixture.

Add the egg whites to a second large bowl and slowly beat them until they are light and fluffy. Here you are trying to introduce as much air as possible into the egg whites so your cake will be light and fluffy. Slowly add the remaining sugar to the egg whites and continue beating the mixture.

When you are satisfied with the airy consistency of your egg whites/sugar, slowly introduce them into your original batter, folding them into the other mixture. You don't want to do this all at once; you want to add the egg whites in two or three different batches, maintaining the airy consistency of the egg whites/sugar.

Once your batter is mixed to your satisfaction, pour it onto the jellyroll pan as evenly as possible. If the batter does not pour out evenly, you can smooth it down with a spatula, but do so lightly. Do not press down on the batter; keep as much air in it as possible.

Bake the cake for about twelve minutes. When pressed on, the cake should have a bouncy give to it. While the cake is baking, spread the clean kitchen towel onto a countertop and sprinkle generously with powdered sugar. When the cake is done baking, invert the cake onto the towel; in other words, you should be able to see the bottom of the pan and not the cake when you set it down on the towel. The cake should fall free of the pan, with the parchment paper remaining on the cake.

Remove the pan, then slowly peel the parchment paper off the cake. Discard the paper and begin rolling the cake up with the towel. This is done to get your cake used to being in log form. It's very important that this is done while the cake is still hot out of the oven. Your log will hold its shape better if it's rolled up while still warm.

Once the cake has cooled, unroll it and spread the peanut butter onto it. I don't go crazy with the filling; you just want to coat the cake with your filling. Since you'll be adding a lot of frosting next, you don't want to add too much sweet stuff to the cake.

Once the filling is spread onto the cake, roll the cake back up carefully. It's possible that no matter how careful you are, your cake will tear a little bit. Don't worry about it! Your frosting will cover any tears, and a small rip or tear here and there won't change the taste or appearance of your cake.

> The easiest effect to add to your Christmas log is "snow," using a bar of white chocolate & a cheese grater.

After the cake has been rolled up, generously frost the cake using a spatula. There are some who prefer to only frost the top and sides of the cake, leaving the ends free of frosting so people can see the "swirls" inside of the cake. That's a matter of personal preference, so do as you wish. When my cake doesn't look all that great on the ends in its rolled form, I add frosting to cover them up. When the swirled filling looks exceptional, I like to show it off. To create the appearance of bark on your cake, add lots of lines and ridges to the frosting with the edge of your spatula.

The easiest effect to add to your Christmas log is "snow," using a bar of white chocolate and a cheese grater. Simply grate the white chocolate bar over the top of the log and you'll get a lovely snow effect. Be sure to get some of the white chocolate over the entire plate you serve your Christmas log on, too! It adds to the snow effect.

Marzipan Recipe

Marzipan is ridiculously easy to make and requires only five ingredients. It can be made a number of different ways, but I like this recipe because it doesn't require any cooking.

You Will Need:

- 1 cup blanched almond flour
- 2 cups powdered sugar
- ¼ teaspoon almond extract
- 1 tablespoon corn syrup
- ¼ cup water
- Colorful icing for decorating (optional)—The colors depend on what you choose to make with the marzipan.

chapter four

Start by mixing the blanched almond flour and powdered sugar in a large bowl. In a separate bowl, mix together the almond extract and corn syrup. Slowly add this mixture to the dry ingredients and mix together using your hands. In order to get a solid dough-like consistency, slowly add some water to the mixture; generally you'll only need 1–2 tablespoons of water, and the less you add the better. Once your marzipan reaches the desired consistency, roll it into a log shape and get creative!

Using the marzipan, you can craft all sorts of interesting things to spruce up your Christmas log. Flowers and mushrooms are the most traditional items, but snowpeople are another easy idea. It's up to you. You can then decorate your marzipan sculptures with icing, making them sweeter and more colorful.

• EXERCISE 18 •
Make a Tió de Nadal (Pooping Christmas Log)

One of the strangest Yuletide traditions is one part Yule log, one part gift-giver, and one part holiday pooper. The *Tió de Nadal* (which translates as "Christmas Log"), or *Caga Tió* ("Poop Log"), hails from Spain's Catalonia region and poops out small presents and treats every Christmas (or Christmas Eve) after being beaten with heated sticks.

During the holiday season, the Tió is treated like a member of the family and is even fed every night from December 8 (the Feast of the Immaculate Conception) until Christmas. In some households, the Christmas Log even grows over the two weeks that it's fed, with the parents replacing it every few days with a larger one.

The Tió is an especially festive Yuletide character and is most often depicted with a giant smile on its face. It's customary to keep a blanket on the Christmas Log so it's comfortable and also because the blanket makes a great place to hide the presents that the Tió is said to defecate out. Traditionally in Catalonia, children prayed to God in their rooms, asking the Christmas Log for an abundance of presents on December 24 or 25 (depending on family tradition). Once the children completed their prayers, they would rush to the Tió and beat it with sticks warmed in the fire, urging it to poop out small gifts and treats to be shared with the entire family.

The Tió in my house doesn't poop out any presents, but we do keep one under our Yule tree just because it's such a festive and fun figure to have around during the holidays. It's also a great conversation piece! Making a Christmas Log is easy, too, because the Tió sits up on just two front legs; the area where its hindquarters would be is generally covered up by its blanket.

Materials Needed:

- A round log, about 6–7 inches in circumference (or bigger or smaller, depending on personal preference)
- Sandpaper
- Pencil
- Acrylic paint or markers
- Sealer
- 2 strong, short sticks or wooden dowels, about an inch in circumference and anywhere from 2–4 inches long (The sticks or dowels you use here should be the same length. During a walk in the woods, I once found a fairly straight six-inch stick and cut it evenly in half to use for the legs.)
- A hammer and 2 strong nails OR an electric drill and 2 screws OR a hot glue gun
- 2 googly eyes, available at most craft stores (optional)
- A small button for the nose (optional)
- Wood glue
- A small Santa hat (optional)

- Decorative fabric or a small blanket, long enough to cover the back half of your Tió and drape down far enough to cover up any small gifts you might want to hide under it

Start by sanding the front of your log with sandpaper. You'll want the front of the log smooth enough that you can easily draw on it with a pencil. Once it's smooth, design the face of your Tió using a pencil. You can create the face of your Christmas Log with markers or paint, though paint will give you the best results. You can use paint to create every aspect of the log's face, or you can glue on eyes and a nose using wood glue. If you are going to glue on body parts, save that step for later. To ensure your Tió's good looks long into the future, spray its face with a paint sealer after the paint or marker dries.

This is completely optional, but if you've got a good sense of humor, you can also draw a butt on your Tió's backside. If you go this route, sand the backside of the log, then paint it using a flesh-colored paint. Adding a butt crack simply requires a slightly curved black line down the middle. Finish with paint sealer.

Once the paint on your Tió is dry, you'll want to attach the legs. The easiest way to attach the legs is to simply hammer them into place with two short but thick nails (one nail per leg). You'll have to hammer them in at a bit of an angle, so watch your fingers while doing this! If you have access to an electric drill, you can simply drill two holes sized for whatever you are using for the legs. Another easy way to add the legs is with a hot glue gun. If the nails or glue can be seen after adding the legs, they can easily be hidden by gluing a bit of holiday greenery around the bits you want to hide. (A little piece from a branch of your Christmas tree should do the trick!)

Note: If you use wooden dowels for the legs, you'll probably want to paint them a color that matches your log before attaching them.

Once the legs are securely attached, finish crafting the Tió's face if you are gluing items onto it. This is also the time to glue a hat onto your log if you so desire. The traditional blanket or fabric used to keep the Tió warm can be glued onto your log or simply draped over its back. Mine is glued on so I don't have to hunt for the blanket every year. Once your Tió is warm in its blanket, it's ready for holiday pooping or whatever other use you might have for it. Traditionally, the Tió poops out hazelnuts, candy, small toys, and *torrone*, a nougat candy made of honey.

Holly

Holly grows as both a bush and a tree and has been popular at winter celebrations for millennia. It was used by the Romans at Saturnalia before being adopted by Christians as a decoration at Christmas. There are several species of holly, with all of them retaining their green leaves and red berries in the winter. If you've ever pricked your finger while handling a holly bush, you are familiar with English holly, the most popular type used in holiday decorating.

Holly has been valued for its magical properties for centuries. In Celtic Gaul, a sprig of holly worn on one's person or fashioned into a crown was thought to keep away malicious spirits. In England, holly was seen as a deterrent against malevolent demons and witches and was often tied to bedposts for protection. Simply decorating with holly can add a little extra protective magic to your home or work and protects against fires, bad weather, and even the evil eye! (I suggest placing a fresh branch of holly above the front door from late November through the start of the new year.) Burning holly on

Christmas Day is said to result in pleasant dreams and a healthier new year.

Holly can also be used for divination. Picking nine holly berries on the Friday night before Christmas, then tying them into a bundle and sleeping with them under one's pillow is said to reveal one's future spouse. Because there are many different types of holly, the first variety brought into one's house can be used to predict who in the household will have the most luck in the coming year. The softer "smooth"-leaf hollies are thought of as female, and if they make their way into a home first at Yuletide, the lady of the house will be especially blessed. The more dangerous "sharp" hollies are generally thought of as male, and their arrival first will benefit the menfolk.

Poinsettia

The poinsettia was first introduced to the United States in 1825 by Dr. Joel Roberts Poinsett, who was the first US Minister to Mexico at the time. (You can see where the plant gets its name obviously.) Poinsett was no doubt struck by the plant's bright red leaves at Yuletide and its use in Mexican churches at Christmas. (Red is the most popular color for poinsettia leaves, but they can also be white, pink, or even striped.) Poinsettias have been a part

Most Popular Yuletide Recordings

Since 2011 *Billboard Magazine* has been keeping track of the most played and streamed holiday tunes on the radio and the internet, and since then, Mariah Carey's "All I Want for Christmas Is You" has claimed the top spot.

Most of the "Holiday Top Ten" is dominated by classics from the 1940s, '50s and '60s, including "Jingle Bell Rock" (1957) by Bobby Helms, "It's the Most Wonderful Time of the Year" (1963) by Andy Williams, "Rockin' Around the Christmas Tree" (1958) by Brenda Lee, "A Holly Jolly Christmas" (1964) by Burl Ives, "The Christmas Song" (1946) by Nat King Cole, "Rudolph the Red-Nosed Reindeer" (1949) and "Here Comes Santa Claus" (1947) by Gene Autry, and "Let It Snow! Let It Snow! Let It Snow!" (1959) by Dean Martin. "Last Christmas," released in 1984 by the English pop band Wham!, is the second youngest recording on the list.

of Mexican Christmas traditions since the 1600s, and before that they were used by the Aztecs for a variety of purposes, most notably as medicine and as a clothing dye.

There are two Mexican folktales featuring the poinsettia. In the most well-known one, a young boy visiting church on Christmas Eve can only find weeds to bring as an offering. After he arrives at church, the weeds are magically turned into poinsettias by a young Jesus thankful for the gift. In another story featuring the poinsettia, a young girl brings weeds as a gift for the baby Jesus in Bethlehem, which are then turned into poinsettias. (How a Mexican plant reaches the Middle East is not addressed in the tale.) I like to think that poinsettias prove that even the most humble and inexpensive gift has the potential for true beauty.

Poinsettias are often thought to be poisonous, especially to cats and dogs, but they are essentially harmless. About the worst thing that will happen to someone (or a pet) after eating a poinsettia is an upset stomach or perhaps diarrhea. Poinsettias are sometimes called *Christmas stars* due to the tendency of their leaves to arrange themselves in star patterns. In Spanish, the poinsettia is known as *la flor de Nochebuena*, the "flower of the Holy Night."

Mistletoe

Mistletoe has been a part of winter decorating since Saturnalia. Its green leaves and red and white berries made it a welcome sight in homes throughout Europe in December. Mistletoe has long been associated with pagan deities, Druids, and magic, but its use as a love plant is a much more recent invention.

According to the Roman historian Pliny the Elder (c. 23–79 CE), mistletoe was the sacred plant among the Druids of Gaul, especially when it was found upon an oak tree. Mistletoe is an abundant enough plant, but it rarely grows on oak trees, making any found there especially sacred. Pliny's Druids also revered the oak tree, so finding mistletoe and oak together was thought to be especially magical.

In an especially striking passage in his work *The Natural History*, Pliny recounts a tale of Druids in white robes gathering around an oak tree for the harvest of their sacred plant. They would use golden sickles to cut down the mistletoe, which was gathered into a white cloth. A sacrifice of two bulls was brought to the gathering, along with a full meal for all involved in the harvest of the mistletoe. (This was obviously a big event.) To amplify the mistletoe's healing power, the plant could be collected only on the sixth night after a new moon. Pliny's story is engaging, but he was not always reliable as a historian, so it's unknown whether this tale is true or not. But even if just a part of it is, it's likely that at least some among the ancient Celts revered mistletoe.

Using Pliny's account as a starting point, it's become popular to believe that the Druids of Gaul (and, by extension, Great Britain) harvested their mistletoe on the Winter Solstice. Pliny's text does not support the idea, but it's something shared year after year near Yuletide. Pliny's assertion that mistletoe was used for healing does have a strong basis in fact. Mistletoe, despite its reputation for being especially poisonous, has been used in European folk medicine for hundreds of years, and some studies show that it might be useful in the fight against cancer. Children and pets should not consume mistletoe, but eating a leaf or a couple of berries won't kill anyone with a healthy immune system (though it might make your tummy upset).

In Norse mythology, mistletoe doesn't act as a healer; it's a killer. After securing a pledge from every living thing not to harm her son Baldur, the goddess Frigg neglected to make the harmless mistletoe plant take a similar oath.

Armed with this knowledge, the trickster god Loki fashioned a dart out of mistletoe and convinced the blind god Hod to throw it at Baldur. I'm guessing the Vikings didn't do a lot of kissing underneath the mistletoe!

Christians have justified the use of mistletoe at Christmas with the claim that the ancient Celts saw mistletoe as symbolic of peace. That's certainly possible, though there's no corroborative evidence suggesting it's true. It's likely that mistletoe became a part of Christmas decorations because it was green in December and was used by the Romans. For many modern Pagans, mistletoe at Yuletide represents rebirth and nature's promise of renewal. The red and white berries symbolize menstrual blood and semen, and its green leaves represent all the life soon to be reborn in the spring.

Today's use of mistletoe as a doorway hanging to let one steal a kiss most likely developed out of a couple of traditions. During the Middle Ages, families would often hang a depiction of the Nativity decorated with winter greenery from their ceilings; this became a popular spot for kissing. Over time, Jesus and his parents were

For many modern Pagans, mistletoe at Yuletide represents rebirth and nature's promise of renewal.

removed from the structure and it came to be known as the *kissing bush* or *kissing bough*. The bush was decorated with evergreen branches, holly, fruit, and of course mistletoe. Eventually the other decorations began to fall away and all that was left was the mistletoe. By the end of the nineteenth century, kissing under the mistletoe had become an extremely popular custom in England and the United States, and it gradually spread around the world in subsequent years.

During the nineteenth century in England, it was thought that the power of the mistletoe to steal kisses waned over time. After each kiss, one of the red berries was taken from the mistletoe, with the kisses ceasing after all the red berries had been harvested. Eventually this custom fell away as well, and most boughs of mistletoe are sold without any berries at all.

I've always been a fan of having a sprig of mistletoe in my kitchen doorway, but mistletoe is not an invitation to take advantage of someone. The only time kisses should be exchanged is when they are consensual (and no one has a cold!). At our house, we simply wish "Yuletide blessings unto you!" to most of our friends when meeting them under the mistletoe.

chapter four

• EXERCISE 19 •
A Mistletoe Sachet

Because of mistletoe's status as the kissing plant, it's a great magical item to keep on your person if you find yourself having to attend a holiday function that's a bit less than loving. For me, this sometimes means family gatherings with disagreeable relatives or perhaps a work party with colleagues I don't get along with. Keeping a little bit of extra magical mistletoe in my pocket reminds me to love, or at least not to get too upset by unpleasant folks.

For This Exercise You Will Need:

- A square of (preferably) white cloth
- Mistletoe with at least one white and one red berry and some leaves
- 3 pieces of string or thread: one green, one white, and one red

Place the white cloth upon your working space and think for a moment about how the ancient Druids once harvested mistletoe in their white robes and used it to heal the ills of their people. Think about how your mistletoe will be used to heal the ills of social functions and bring a bit of peace to contentious spaces.

Place the leaves of your mistletoe (dry or fresh) on the white cloth and say:

Leaf of mistletoe green,
Keep this Yuletide serene.
Berry of brilliant red,
No tears or anger shed.
Berry of blazing white,
To all a good and quiet night!

Bundle up your leaves and berries and tie up your sachet with the three strings, reciting the following lines with the appropriate colors. Be sure to make a good, strong knot with each string to keep your mistletoe safe. Knots are also great at keeping magical energy in place, which is what you want here.

A string of green to keep the peace,
A string of white so strife will cease,
A string of red for understanding,
Tied all together to begin the enchanting!

Carry your sachet of mistletoe anyplace you go where you might run into people who are a bit less than polite.

Nutcracker

Visit any department store during Yuletide and you'll inevitably encounter a large collection of decorative nutcrackers. Working nutcrackers began to be associated with the holiday season during the late seventeenth century in Germany and became popular throughout Europe and later North America over the next two hundred years. The exact reason that nutcrackers became popular in late December is an open question. It might simply be because they make attractive gifts, or because nuts, as a symbol of fruitfulness, were popular in many areas of Europe near Yule. Traditionally, nutcrackers resemble soldiers, though they are available in a variety of styles today (and are generally decorative; despite their moving mouths, most of them would have trouble smashing a blueberry).

Nutcrackers today are generally associated with the ballet *The Nutcracker Suite*, which features a score from Russian composer Pyotr Ilyich Tchaikovsky (1840–1893). Tchaikovsky's score is an inescapable part of the season, and compositions such as the "Dance of the Sugar Plum Fairy," "Waltz of the Flowers," and "March of the Nutcracker" are as familiar to most of us as "Jingle Bells"

TIP 10

✴

Reuse and Recycle

New does not necessarily mean better, and it almost always means more expensive. Instead of buying new items or just throwing things away, reuse and recycle!

Last year's holiday cards can be used to make fabulous and colorful gift tags for presents. Want to make them even fancier? Cut the cards with a pair of edging scissors to give your gift tags wavy, artful edges. Add some sparkle to your tags with a glitter glue pen.

While searching for new Yuletide decorations, be sure to visit secondhand stores. Buying a used ornament or decoration not only will save you a lot of money but will also keep a usable item out of the local landfill! Many secondhand stores even sell complete artificial trees for a fraction of what you'd spend at a department store or online.

every December. The story told in the ballet is a rather simple one, featuring a girl named Clara who receives a beautiful nutcracker as a gift on Christmas Eve. After her family has gone to bed, Clara goes to visit her present and finds herself in the middle of a battle between an army of mice and an army of gingerbread men led by her nutcracker. Clara distracts the leader of the mice by throwing her shoe, allowing the nutcracker to mortally wound his foe. The nutcracker then whisks Clara away to a magical land and everyone lives happily ever after.

The original version of *The Nutcracker* (titled *The Nutcracker and the Mouse King*) was written in 1816 by the Prussian (modern Germany) author E. T. A. Hoffmann (1776–1822). Hoffmann's short story is far more violent than the version most of us know from the ballet and has mostly been overshadowed by dancing sugar plum fairies. In 1844 the French novelist Alexandre Dumas (1829–1869) released a more child-friendly version of Hoffmann's story, which became the basis of the ballet. Though the ballet version of *The Nutcracker* is wildly popular today, it was not successful when it was first performed in 1892 and would not become a staple of the season until the 1950s.

Chestnut Divination

Chestnuts have been a staple of European diets for thousands of years and have been a part of many Yuletide celebrations for much of that time. Chestnuts were one of the most popular holiday foods in the early United States and were consumed on their own and in stuffing and other dishes. In the early twentieth century, most American chestnut trees died of blight, and the nut began to decline in popularity, but not before being immortalized in the 1946 tune "A Christmas Song" with the line "chestnuts roasting on an open fire."

Today, chestnuts are still immensely popular in Europe at Yuletide and can be found roasting on just about every busy street corner in Northern Europe. (In the United States, the custom of outdoor chestnut roasting remains popular in New York City and other spots in the Northeast.) Italy has become the primary exporter of chestnuts in the world, and most bags of chestnuts from the grocery store come from there. Chestnuts have a musky, earthy flavor, and most people find them more palatable as an ingredient in cakes, sauces, and stuffing than as a treat straight from the oven.

Nuts have a long history of being used to help individuals gauge the strength of a relationship. Because chestnuts are so readily associated with Yuletide, they are perfect for catching a glimpse of the future in December.

For This Exercise You Will Need:

- Some (unroasted) chestnuts
- A fire in the fireplace or a frying pan with a see-through (glass) lid

If you want the nuts to inform you of the state of a relationship, take two chestnuts and designate one for yourself and one for the person you are curious about. Place both nuts in the fire and securely close the screen that prevents sparks from popping out of the fire and onto the floor. (This is especially important because chestnuts can explode!) If the two chestnuts burn slowly next to each other, your relationship is secure. If one burns hotter than the other, the person whose chestnut is burning brighter cares more about the relationship. If one of the chestnuts explodes, then that individual will be the reason the relationship fails.

For those without access to a roaring fire, this divination can also be done in a frying pan with some adjustments.

Warm up the pan on medium-high heat (cast iron works best but is not necessary), then drop in your chestnuts and place a lid on the pan. If the two chestnuts roast evenly, which takes about fifteen minutes, the relationship is strong. If one roasts faster than the other, then one individual values the relationship more than the other. And, not surprisingly, if one of the chestnuts explodes, the person represented by that nut will be the relationship's doom!

If you just want to roast some chestnuts to eat, rinse the nuts and then score the flat side of each chestnut with a large *X* to keep it from blowing up. Place the nuts on a cookie sheet (*X*-side up) and roast in the oven for twenty-five minutes at 350° Fahrenheit. After removing them from the oven, let them cool for a few minutes before peeling away the shells and eating. If there's a fire in the fireplace (a bed of coals works best), repeat the steps above and place your chestnuts in a cast-iron skillet or the shovel you use to scoop out the fireplace ashes. Place your pan or shovel full of chestnuts on the coals and close your fire screen. After twenty-five minutes or so, you should have roasted and edible chestnuts.

Traditions Around the Tube

Like many children born during the second half of the twentieth century, I grew up at least partially around the television, and there was no better time of year for TV shows than December! Cartoons in prime time! It was the kind of magick that only happened with any real regularity at Christmas. And weirdly, I can't picture my living room during Yuletide without a couple of cartoons on the TV. To this day, seeing *Rudolph* every year is just as important to me as putting up a Yule tree.

Animated holiday specials have become so ingrained in our culture that their soundtracks are played in department stores, and ornaments featuring Rudolph and Charlie Brown hang on millions of Christmas trees. Let's take a look at a few of the most influential holiday cartoons, most of which still air on network television decades after they were created.

Rudolph the Red-Nosed Reindeer (1964)

Based on a poem written by Robert L. May and then a song by Johnny Marks, *Rudolph the Red-Nosed Reindeer* might be the most well-loved of all holiday specials. Bumbles, elves who want to be dentists, and the song "Holly Jolly Christmas" have all become readily identifiable parts of the holiday season, and they all come from *Rudolph*. Even today, this remains one of the most watched TV shows airing on network television every December.

A Charlie Brown Christmas (1965)

While most animated holiday offerings are more fanciful than religious, *A Charlie Brown Christmas* is a big exception. Featuring a long quote from the New Testament's Gospel of Luke by the blanket-loving Linus, this might be the only truly popular Christmas cartoon to specifically name-check Jesus. Even with the strong religious message, it's focus on a simpler holiday season still rings true for many of us. The musical score by jazz pianist Vince Guaraldi (1928–1976) is perhaps even more popular than the cartoon and is impossible to escape during the holidays.

How the Grinch Stole Christmas (1966)

The original Frankenstein's monster, actor Boris Karloff stars as the voice of the Grinch in this holiday classic. Though Dr. Seuss's beloved book has been adapted three times and counting now, the original 1966 version remains the favorite of most anyone under the age of ten (and probably their parents, too!).

Frosty the Snowman (1969)

With his magical silk hat and a corncob pipe, Frosty has become one of the archetypal figures of the holiday season. Based on the 1950 song of the same name, the original *Frosty* cartoon went on to inspire several sequels, including one with Rudolph in 1979.

Santa Claus Is Coming to Town (1970)

Animation studio Rankin/Bass is responsible for everything on this list but *A Charlie Brown Christmas* and *The Grinch*, which makes it surprising that it took them until 1970 to get to the origins of Santa Claus. The 1974 sequel, *A Year Without a Santa Claus*, might be even better, featuring an in-command Mrs. Claus, along with the weather-god Miser Brothers (Snow Miser and Heat Miser) and their mom, Mother Nature herself!

Chapter Five
NEW YEAR'S AND BEYOND

I t has become more and more common to see our Yuletide festivities end immediately after the Winter Solstice and Christmas. Many of the stores I shop at start
putting up displays on December 26 for Valentine's Day,
which is over a month and a half away! I find this especially tragic because the phrase "Happy holidays" was
designed to include the secular celebration of New Year's
and, in many places, the continued Yuletide celebrations
of Epiphany and Twelfth Night.

The popular song "The Twelve Days of Christmas" was written to commemorate the Yuletide season that begins on December 25 and runs through January 5. No traditional holiday celebration is complete without a bit of festive activity in early January. In fact, New Year's Eve and New Year's Day, along with the celebrations observed in the days afterward, have been an integral and influential part of the Yuletide season for thousands of years.

New Year's Celebrations

Though Saturnalia tends to get the most attention at Yuletide, the celebration of the January Kalends was just as important in the Roman Empire. The January Kalends were in many ways an extension of Saturnalia, featuring many of the same decorations and the exchange of presents. The month of January was also sacred to the Roman god Janus, a god of doorways, time, endings, and new beginnings. Janus is also the source of the word *January*.

January 1 has been recognized as the start of the new year since 46 CE and the adoption of the Julian calendar, devised by the Roman politician and general Julius Caesar (100–44 BCE). During Caesar's time, Roman consuls were generally installed on January 1, making the day especially festive and significant. Though established during the pagan Roman Empire (and under a pagan Roman leader), January 1 has long been a secular start to a new calendar year and has remained so for over two thousand years. Several religious and spiritual traditions have their own start to the new year too, and that's great! There's nothing wrong with celebrating more than one.

Many of the things we associate most with Yuletide today once took place on New Year's Eve and New Year's Day in many cultures. During the Middle Ages, New Year's Day was the most popular day to exchange gifts, a tradition that still exists in parts of Greece, France, and Russia. Presents and cards were exchanged on New Year's Day well into the nineteenth century in parts of Great Britain, Canada, and the United States. Gifts received on New Year's Day were still generally called Christmas presents, because Christmas was observed as an entire season and not as one day. In areas where gifts were exchanged on January 1, early printed versions of *A Visit from St. Nicholas (The Night Before Christmas)* often had the last line changed to "Happy New Year to all, and to all a good night!" instead of the more familiar "Merry Christmas to all …"

As Christmas evolved into a holiday about families and staying indoors, the more rambunctious and social elements of the Yuletide season migrated to New Year's Eve.

chapter five

Unlike Christmas, New Year's is a social holiday, with parties and public gatherings expected by many. A million people congregate in New York City's Times Square for the annual "ball drop" on New Year's Eve, a staggering number and a testament to the shared nature of the New Year's holiday. New Year's Eve is also celebrated in many parts of the world with fireworks celebrations both large and small, which is another social event.

• EXERCISE 21 •
Candle Divination

An old German folk custom on New Year's Eve uses molten lead as a way to peek into the future. A small amount of lead is melted and then dropped into a bowl or cup of cold water. The resulting shape of the lead is then interpreted to see what the new year holds. Most of us don't have lead at the ready to melt on New Year's Eve, but we probably do have candles, which can be easily substituted.

For This Exercise You Will Need:

- A long taper candle (Be sure to avoid "dripless" candles, since it's the drips that are most important here!)

- A large bowl of cold water

To begin, light the candle and let it burn for at least a minute while thinking about the year ahead. When you feel ready to look into the future, pour the wax from your candle into the water and say:

Wax into water, candle glow in the night,
Grant to me the gift of the second sight.
Bring this year's future out into the light!

Let the wax drip into the water for at least twenty seconds before placing the candle in a candleholder or other secure space. Now look at the wax drippings in the bowl while letting your mind wander. Does that bit of wax look like a dollar sign? Perhaps more money will come into your life this year. Is that a heart? Perhaps true love will be found! Write down your interpretations of the candle wax and then compare your interpretations to what actually happens later in the year.

This exercise makes a great game to play at New Year's parties. It's especially fun to get a lot of people to offer their own individual interpretations of the wax. If playing with a large group of people, you'll have to fish all of the individual pieces of wax out of the bowl before the next person pours their wax into the bowl. The more you

chapter five

practice this exercise, the easier it gets to spot the shapes, forms, and premonitions that can be found in the candle wax. Before your New Year's Eve gets too wild, be sure to extinguish the candles when you're done playing.

Hoppin' John on New Year's Day

In many parts of the American South, it's traditional to eat black-eyed peas on New Year's Day for good luck in the coming year. The exact reason for this has been lost to history, though theories abound. Black-eyed peas might have been the first food eaten by newly freed slaves when the Emancipation Proclamation went into effect on January 1, 1863 (certainly a cause for celebration!). Others trace the custom of black-eyed peas on New Year's Day to the American Civil War. According to this theory, black-eyed peas and salted pork were the only foodstuffs not taken by Union (Yankee) soldiers, and their presence allowed Confederate soldiers to survive with meager supplies.

The most likely reason for the popularity of black-eyed peas at New Year's is simply that they grow in many parts of the American South during the winter. They were also a relatively cheap (and healthy) foodstuff and therefore were popular both before and after the Civil War.

Eventually the custom spread throughout the South and to many other parts of the country.

Most people who observe the custom think that eating black-eyed peas is enough to ensure at least a little bit of luck, but there are some extended superstitions associated with the custom. Some folks believe that a person must eat 365 peas on New Year's Day to ensure an entire year's worth of luck. If they eat only 200 peas, they'll have only 200 days with good luck! Leaving uneaten peas on your plate is also considered bad luck, so avoid putting more on your plate than you can comfortably eat. I think the magical power of the black-eyed pea comes from its "eye," which reflects negativity.

Black-eyed peas do not have a particularly strong flavor, but for people who didn't grow up eating them, they are often an acquired taste. To make them a bit more palatable, serve them as Hoppin' John, which adds a touch of spice and a lot of extra flavor.

To Make Hoppin' John You Will Need:

- 16 ounces black-eyed peas, frozen or dried
- 6 slices thick-cut bacon, diced (Ham or sausage can be substituted here, but the bacon fat adds a lot of flavor to the beans.)

- ¼ cup diced onion (optional)
- ½ cup white rice
- 1 cup water, for the rice (If you're using instant rice, you'll need only ½ cup water.)
- ¼ teaspoon cayenne pepper (more or less to taste)
- ¼ teaspoon salt (more or less to taste)
- ¼ teaspoon black pepper (more or less to taste)

Black-eyed peas typically take up to an hour to prepare, whether frozen or dried. Start by boiling the peas until they are soft, usually at least 45 minutes. For a bit of extra flavor, boil the peas in chicken or vegetable stock. After the peas are cooked, drain and set aside.

Once your black-eyed peas are prepared, place the diced bacon in a frying pan and cook until crispy. If you are using onions, cook them with the bacon until the onions are soft. In a pot or large saucepan, combine all of the ingredients and let simmer for about half an hour (or until all the water is absorbed by the rice). I suggest making sure that all the bacon fat goes into your pot for maximum deliciousness.

If you want to make your Hoppin' John a bit more special, you can add a clean coin to the pot or saucepan while the dish simmers. Whoever finds the coin in their meal will be especially blessed in the coming year. If you choose to go this route, be sure to use a large coin (at least the size of an American quarter) so no one accidentally swallows it. Silver is also nice and shiny and should be seen easily by everyone eating. Put a little extra magic in your coin by saying a quick blessing over it before tossing it into the pot:

Luck to me and mine,
Wealth, health, love, and wine.
To the one who finds this token,
This spell will not be broken!

To make the meal as magical as possible, serve your Hoppin' John with corn bread and collard greens. Corn bread is considered a lucky food because of its golden color. Based on the belief that "like attracts like," perhaps corn bread's golden color will bring some of that precious metal into your life, or at least a little sunshine. Collard greens are considered lucky because they are the same color as American money. Eat some greens to get a little green!

Lucky New Year's Day Food

In addition to black-eyed peas, greens, and corn bread, there are several other foods that are thought to bring luck when eaten on New Year's Eve or Day.

GRAPES: Eating twelve grapes at the stroke of midnight on New Year's Eve is said to ensure good luck in the new year. This is more challenging than it sounds, because you are supposed to eat one grape each time the clock strikes.

POMEGRANATE: In Greece, families routinely break pomegranates upon their kitchen floors at midnight on New Year's Eve. The more seeds that fall out of the fruit, the better and more prosperous the new year is thought to be. Seeds, of course, represent new life and abundance, though it might be easier to just cut open a pomegranate and share some of the seeds with friends!

PORK: In many parts of Europe, pork is eaten on New Year's Day because pigs can only look forward. (Have you ever seen a pig look over its shoulder?) Fresh pork has long been considered a luxury good, so eating it is also seen as a way to attract wealth and power.

TIP 11
✦
Auld Lang Syne

The poem "Auld Lang Syne" by the Scottish writer Robert Burns (1959–1796) has become synonymous with New Year's Eve and is sung by many in Great Britain and North America every year at the stroke of midnight. The Scots-language phrase "auld lang syne" signifies the days that are now behind us. Not surprisingly, much of the poem features references to drinking, always a popular Yuletide activity. Though attributed to Robert Burns, the first stanza derives from an earlier Scottish song now lost to history.

Curiously, "Auld Lang Syne" was not always associated with New Year's. Postcards at the start of the twentieth century often used the phrase as a Halloween greeting! It was also sung at Christmas and is still performed at weddings, funerals, and graduations in many parts of Great Britain.

FISH: Don't like pork? Try fish instead! Fish are representative of the wealth of the sea, and they often travel in schools, which might bring some extra friends into your life in the coming year. The scales are also thought to resemble coins.

CABBAGE: Cabbage has been associated with good health since pagan antiquity and was eaten by both the Greeks and the Egyptians for just that reason. It's still eaten by many on New Year's Day for similar reasons. (Cabbage also grows well in the winter, which is another reason it's popular at New Year's.)

SOBA NOODLES: In Japan, soba noodles slurped at midnight are said to signify a long life. If you can slurp an entire noodle without breaking it, you will live to a very old age.

LENTILS: Italians eat lentils on New Year's Day because they are said to resemble old Roman coins. If this is truly the reason, then this is a very old tradition! Lentils are a popular choice in other parts of the world too and are a part of New Year's Day dining in Brazil, Hungary, the Czech Republic, and France.

ROUND-SHAPED PASTRIES OR CAKES: Having everything "come full circle" in life is considered a positive development, and round cakes (even doughnuts!) symbolize just that. Most people also simply like cakes and other sweet pastries.

Twelfth Night and the Twelve Days of Christmas

Largely forgotten today, especially in the United States, Twelfth Night was once the crown jewel of the Yuletide season. Gift-giving, Misrule, masquerades, wassailing, and mummery were all once the province of Twelfth Night— the climax of an extended Yuletide celebration that lasted from Christmas Eve all the way through January 6. Twelfth Night as a holiday hasn't entirely disappeared, as versions of it are still celebrated in many parts of Europe and Latin America, but it's importance in the larger scheme of Yuletide celebrations is generally overlooked.

Traditionally, Twelfth Night commemorates the final night of the "Twelve Days of Christmas," which begin on Christmas Eve. The Twelve Days of Christmas aren't just about the twelve consecutive days that begin on December 25 and end on January 6; this period is also about the twelve *nights* that run from December 24 through

January 5. It was at night that many of the most festive Yuletide traditions were celebrated, and as the last night of the season, Twelfth Night was often the best party of the season. Twelfth Day was still a holiday worthy of celebration, but it also marked the end of the season—probably best not to do too much drinking before returning to work.

As discussed in chapter 1, January 6 is most often celebrated today as Epiphany and commemorates the arrival of the Magi, or Three Wise Men, in Bethlehem to visit the baby Jesus. For this reason, the holiday is often known as Three Kings' Day. Because the Three Kings, or Wise Men, have always been known as gift-givers, Epiphany became a popular day to exchange gifts. In Spain and many parts of Latin America, Epiphany, or *Día de los Reyes*, remains an important day for gift-giving, with the Wise Men serving as the gift-givers.

Just how the Wise Men pass out gifts varies across the globe. In the Philippines, children leave out their shoes to be filled with gifts and candy. In Puerto Rico, many children spend January 5 gathering up grass for the Three Wise Men's camels and then placing it in a shoebox so it can be picked up by the Magi and shared with their camels. In Belgium, children dress up as the Three Kings and go door to door looking for treats. One of the strangest gift-giving rituals on Epiphany is the handing out of cigarettes in Portugal to both children (as young as five) and adults to smoke.

Interestingly enough, the first celebrations of Epiphany were not about the Three Wise Men or the days after Jesus's birth, but instead were about Jesus's baptism by the prophet John the Baptist thirty years later.

The Magi, or Three Wise Men

The Three Wise Men, also known as the Three Kings or the Magi, are some of the most recognizable figures of the Yuletide season. The Gospel of Matthew (the only book in the Bible to feature an appearance by the supposed trio) says very little about the Wise Men, but only that they were "magi," followed a magical star to the location of Jesus, and gave him gifts of frankincense, gold, and myrrh. There is no information about their place of origin or even their exact number.

The term *magi* generally refers to priests of the Zoroastrian religion from Persia and is often translated as "astrologer." If the Magi were following a star, it is even more likely that they were astrologers by profession. *Magi* is also related to the word *magus*, which is generally used to indicate a user of magic. For this reason, the Magi make frequent appearances in magical grimoires and on magical items such as candles, incense, and powders.

Although the Christian Bible does not indicate just how many Magi there were, the number three is most often used because the group brought three different items with them, and it's assumed that each magus brought one of those items. Because gold, frankincense, and myrrh were all very expensive items two thousand years ago, the Magi are sometimes imagined as kings to explain their wealth.

The Magi make frequent appearances in magical grimoires and on magical items such as candles and incense.

Several centuries after the Gospel of Matthew was written, specific names were attached to the Three Wise Men, along with a distinct place of origin for each one. Caspar was said to be an Indian king, Melchior a Persian one, and Balthasar an Arabian king. This is all very unlikely, but it makes for a good story.

Just as famous as the Magi is the Star of Bethlehem (or Christmas Star). This magical star allegedly guided the Three Wise Men to the site of Jesus's birth, and once it fulfilled its purpose, it then disappeared from the night sky. Since the age of the European Renaissance, astronomers have been looking for an explanation for the star but have had limited success.

For many centuries the most common explanation for the Star of Bethlehem was a comet, often the famous Halley's Comet. Halley's Comet did pass by Earth in the year 12 BCE, but comets were genuinely seen as bad omens at the time of the Roman Empire, and the dates don't quite add up either. (Most scholars think Jesus was born in the year 3 CE.)

The conjunction of various stars and planets has also been suggested as a possible origin story for the Star of Bethlehem. It's important to note that a *conjunction* refers to stars and planets simply being *near* each other in the night sky—they do not necessarily overlap. I think this means it's less likely that such an occurrence would be called a "star," but meaning and context are often lost in translation.

Jupiter and Saturn were very near each other in the night sky in the year 7 BCE, and their conjunction occurred in the constellation of Aquarius. Given Jesus's association with fish (he was called a "fisher of men"), this explanation is at least symbolically interesting. Conjunctions involving

Jupiter and the star Regulus occurred just a few years later, as did a conjunction between Venus and Jupiter.

The Three Wise Men are most likely more myth than flesh-and-blood historical figures. The star they were said to have followed has never been identified, and a star suddenly appearing in the night sky in the days of the Roman Empire would have been a very big story indeed. Their inclusion in the birth narrative of Jesus was likely done to make the argument that Jesus was the true king of the Jewish people, with the star serving as a way to make his birth that much more special.

• EXERCISE 23 •
Twelfth Night Tree Wassail Blessing

Wassailing was a popular pastime on Twelfth Night and was sometimes done to honor the fruit trees (usually apple and pear trees) that provided the wassail. "Wassailing the trees" was said to ensure a good harvest in the new year and rid the trees of any negative spirits that might be dwelling nearby. In certain parts of England, wassail was also given to beehives for similar reasons.

This blessing can be done for a favorite tree, your garden, or even a pot that you grow herbs or tomatoes in.

What's important is to honor the green growing things in your life (wherever they may be) and let them know you look forward to their return and blossoming in the spring. This rite is probably best done in the daytime, hopefully with the sun shining down upon you. The traditional time for performing a blessing of this type was on Twelfth Day, but any time at the start of the new year will work.

For This Exercise You Will Need:

- A nice pot of wassail or some warmed-up apple cider
- A cup or bowl that's important to you (for taking the wassail/cider outside and sharing it with your trees, plants, and/or garden
- A ladle

As your wassail warms up, stir it periodically and say the following blessing over it:

With love and care, this drink I stir,
Growth and blessings from this liquor!
May abundance come from its touch,
The gifts of the world I love so much!

When your wassail is warm, ladle it into the cup or bowl and take it to the spots you wish to bless. If there are several spots you want to bless and your cup isn't all that big, it's perfectly fine to make a few trips in and out, which is especially useful if it's cold on the day of your blessing. As you approach the trees, plants, and places you wish to bless, visualize them full of life, energy, and fruit. Think of them blooming in the spring and the gifts they will give in the summertime.

When you are done with your visualization, pour some of the wassail out onto the ground and say:

By leaf and bud and blossom,
By earth and sun and rain,
I bless this space in the new year,
May it be one of fruit and life and gain!
Let the wassail drive away the dark
And prepare the way for new life.
May the growing season be long and strong,
Free of any pestilence and strife!

If there's snow on the ground where you live, the warm wassail melting the snow is always a welcome sight! Before you leave your tree, pot, or garden spot, thank the tree for its gifts and the earth for its many blessings.

• EXERCISE 24 •
Chalking the Door

Walk past a Catholic church shortly after Three Kings' Day and you're likely to see what looks like a mathematical equation written in chalk on an outside door. Known as "chalking the door," what looks like a math problem is actually a blessing for the new year. Once a common practice in many parts of Europe, chalking the door is less well known in the United States but is still practiced by many churches. Chalking the door has been around for over two thousand years and was first used in Jewish homes to keep out evil spirits and the Angel of Death. (This means it predates its adoption as a practice by the Catholic Church.)

Chalking the door originally was common at both homes and churches, and no matter the location, it was traditionally performed by a priest. Eventually there were too many houses and not enough priests for members of the clergy to oversee every chalking, so now it's just as likely to be done by the residents of a home as by a priest. A chalk blessing can be placed anywhere on the outside of the door, but the most common spot is at the

TIP 12

A More Frugal Yuletide

*Waste Not, Want Not .*The holidays are known for excess, and the biggest overindulgence for many of us at Yuletide occurs at the dinner table. Think about portion sizes and buy and prepare only the amount of food you and your guests can eat. If you do have leftovers, be sure to actually eat them later.

Drive a Little Bit Less. The bustle of the holidays often involves several trips to the grocery store and the mall, and all destinations in between. Before you hop in your car, plan your route and even your week, and minimize side trips. Or better yet, walk or take public transportation to the store if that's an option in your area.

Only Buy Things That Will Be Valued. Resist the urge to buy your loved ones any old thing. Instead, choose practical gifts that will be valued over the long term. If you can't decide what to give someone, try cash, a gift card, or something homemade.

top of the door. When writing out the blessing, I think it's easiest to start either in the middle of the door or on the left-hand side, but you should do whatever feels most comfortable to you.

The traditional formula for a chalk blessing utilizes the Christian cross, which often simply looks like a plus sign (+), as well as the first initials of the Three Wise Men and the year of the blessing. For example, a Catholic chalking their front door in 2022 would write the following formula:

20 ✠ C ✠ M ✠ B ✠ 22

The *20* stands for the century, *C* for Caspar, *M* for Melchior, *B* for Balthasar, and *22* for the specific year. The initials of the Three Wise Men also double as an abbreviation for *Christus mansionem benedicat*, a Latin blessing that translates as "May Christ bless this house." For those with an affinity for Jesus and the Three Wise Men, this formula works great, but I offer some alternatives below.

Before starting, bless your chalk by saying:

I bless and cleanse this chalk. May its magic keep this house and all within it safe from harm in the coming year!

If you've chosen to use some incense, waft the incense smoke around the piece of chalk you'll be writing with. This blessing can be done indoors or out, which is especially useful if someone in your house is allergic to incense.

Once the chalk has been blessed, think about what it is you want to bring into your life over the next year and what you'd like to stay far away. These are the letters I use most often:

H for health and happiness and to keep disease, sickness, and sadness away

W for wealth and to remain relatively prosperous

L for love, so I might continue to love those I care about and be loved in return

F for family, both blood and chosen, and to keep them close to my heart

R for safe return, which is especially useful if someone in the house travels a lot

S for success and to drive away the sloth that often gets in the way of it

Instead of using a cross to link together the letters and numbers, I simply use an ordinary plus sign (+). For me, the plus sign is full of spiritual significance, as I see it as being representative of the yearly turn of the Wheel; and since I want this blessing to last for an entire year, it seems especially appropriate. Personal religious symbols are fine to use here too, if you wish, and will most certainly give your blessing a little extra power and energy.

If you are close to any deities or higher powers, you can also add their first initial to your chalk blessing. For instance, Archangel Michael is known for keeping away evil forces and for being an angel of healing. To keep the fey folk happy and out of your house over the next year, you might add the first initial of the Fairy Queen, generally thought to be Titania. I usually put the names of any deities or higher powers after and before the dates in the formula. For the year 2022 that would mean:

$$20 + M + W + L + S + T + 22$$

The *20* is for the century, *M* for Michael, *W* for wealth, *L* for love, *S* for success, *T* for Titania, and *22* for the year.

When you've decided on the energies you want to bring into (or keep out of) your life this year, write the formula on the door, taking time to verbalize all of your intentions as you do so. For example:

The old year has ended and it's time to once more usher in the new. May the fates smile down upon this home and all who are in it. (Write *20*.)

As you write down the first two numbers of the current year (20), visualize your home in the coming year. See both it and those who reside in it safe and content. If you are calling upon a higher power during your chalk blessing, thank that power now.

Archangel Michael, may your healing energies keep all within healthy and hearty, and may you stand as a ward at our door, driving away all that is baneful. (Write the letter *M*.)

As you write down the qualities you want to bring in and/or keep away over the next year, say a bit about them out loud, and how you hope they'll find their way into the lives of those around you.

In the new year, may this home know only wealth and abundance and be free of want. Let our bellies be full and may we be free of worry over coin or dollar. See that our needs

are taken care of and that we are gracious with the gifts we've received. (Write *W*.)

In the new year, may this home be one of love. May our relationships bloom and the bonds between family and friends only deepen. (Write *L*.)

In the new year, may those of this house know only success. We shall achieve what we set out to do, and all that does not aid us in those pursuits shall stay here on this side of the door. (Write *S*.)

If you are writing down the initial of another deity or power, do this now, inviting their power into your blessing.

Titania, Queen of the Fairies, know that the fair folk are our friends and neighbors. Remind us to love the earth around us and to be a part of this greater world. We pay you and your folk honor and would be spared from any games or tricks. (Write *T*.)

Finish the chalk blessing by writing the two numbers for the year (*22* in this example) and saying the following words:

Blessings be upon us for the new year! May 2022 bring to us all that we ask and may we share those blessings with those around us. Hail the new year! (Write *22*.)

If you have children or simply live with a lot of people, a chalk blessing is extra fun to do with a crowd! Take turns and let everyone say a few words and write a letter or two. Though traditionally performed on Three Kings' Day, this chalk blessing can be performed anytime between January 1 and 6.

Plough Monday

Up until the start of the twentieth century, Yuletide in England generally lasted until the first Monday after Three Kings' Day. That Monday was celebrated as *Plough Monday* and marked the return of both regular work and the planting season in England. Though summer and even spring were still a long way off, there were always chores on the farm to attend to and fields to till and prepare for planting.

In many parts of rural England, Plough Monday was celebrated with a parade. Farmhands and laborers would decorate themselves with bows and ribbons and then drag a plough adorned with flowers and other decorations through town, often collecting either church donations or money for themselves as they went along. Plough Monday parades featured music, dancers, and a character dressed in furs carrying a pig's bladder known as "the Fool" for comic relief. Plough Monday also carried with it the threat of menace, as those too cheap to contribute to the parade financially were threatened with vandalism to their yards with the plough.

Beginning in the nineteenth century, men and boys covered in straw and known as "straw bears" sometimes took part in Plough Monday celebrations. The straw bears became so popular in some areas that they took the place of the ploughs that had previously been the stars of the parade. Straw bears are still a part of Plough celebrations in the English town of Whittlesey today (though the holiday is now celebrated on the first Saturday after January 6). Not surprisingly, Plough Monday celebrations generally ended with large meals and several tankards of ale. These celebrations declined at the start of the twentieth century but have been revived over the past few decades.

• EXERCISE 25 •
Yuletide Remembrance Tree and Ornaments

Yuletide is a joyous celebration for most people these days. There are parties, festive lights, abundant food and drink, gifts, and lots of good cheer. But for our ancestors, Yuletide was a frightening time of year because of the dark and the cold, and ghost stories were once as plentiful as cheerful holiday tales. The darkness that was once a part of the holiday has mostly been swept away, but many of us still feel it keenly, especially when met with remembrances of loved ones who have passed away.

Over the years, many of us have lost people who are dear to us, and oftentimes these individuals played a large role in our holiday celebrations. At Yule, I most keenly feel the absence of my grandparents, two very magical people who shaped my love for the midwinter celebrations. I used to put Yule ornaments honoring them on our (regular) holiday tree, but there was something about setting their picture next to resin casts of Rudolph, Santa Claus, and Spider-Man that just didn't sit right with me. I decided that those whom my wife and I have lost over the years needed their own space, and I found it in what I call a *Remembrance Tree*.

A Remembrance Tree is a place to honor and remember those we've lost over the years: friends, family members, celebrities who might have been influential in our lives, and, of course, our animal companions too. Any extra Christmas tree one might have lying around (artificial or real) makes for an acceptable Remembrance Tree, but I think they are a bit more special when they have their own unique look and feel. For that reason, mine is a do-it-yourself "tree" made from a tomato cage flipped upside down. Unfamiliar with a tomato cage? It's a cone-shaped metal frame placed around a tomato plant while it grows to help the plant hold up its fruit.

To Make This Remembrance Tree You Will Need:

- A tomato cage flipped upside down (The size can vary according to your needs.)
- A zip tie
- A pair of scissors (to cut the zip tie)

Optional Items:

- Lights for the tree (A string of regular Christmas lights works just fine.)
- Garland for decoration
- A small container to set the cage-tree in (This is not really necessary, as a tomato cage will stand just fine on its own. But if you want a bit of extra security, purchase a pot about the same diameter as your tomato cage, fill it with dirt, and set your cage in it.

chapter five

The extra weight will keep the cage from wobbling or tipping over.

A tomato cage flipped upside down is the already the perfect shape to simulate a tree. (In most instances, the loose ends of a tomato cage are placed into the ground around the tomato plant.) The only real work you have to do for this DIY Remembrance Tree is to tie up the three loose ends of the cage. The easiest way to do this is with a zip tie. Simply wrap the zip tie around the loose ends about an inch from the very top. After the zip tie is secure, cut away the excess with the scissors.

Once you've tied up the loose ends, you are free to decorate the tree however you choose. I prefer to keep mine rather spartan, as I want the focus to be on the pictures of those I've lost. To that end, I simply add a small string of lights (50 count) and wrap a few feet of gold garland around the structure of the cage. If you want your cage-tree to look more like a traditional tree, this can be done by buying garland that looks like pine branches and wrapping it around the perimeter of the cage.

The style of ornaments you use for your Remembrance Tree is a personal decision. You can buy empty ornament balls and fill them with pictures of those you've lost and other keepsakes. You can also buy small picture frames and place your photos in them and then hang them on your tree. I like to keep my Remembrance Tree mostly uniform, so I make my ornaments from wood slices and pictures I've printed out from my computer.

To Make Wood-Slice Ornaments You Will Need:

- Pictures of lost loved ones
- Wood slices (These can be purchased online and in craft stores, and they vary in size. I use ones about ½ inch in diameter. Purchased wood slices have the extra benefit of already being smooth and sanded, though you could certainly make your own slices easily enough.)
- Pencil
- Scissors
- Wood glue
- Sealant
- A hand-held drill
- Ribbon
- Ornament hooks or paper clips (optional)

To make your ornaments, start with the pictures of those you've lost. You can use actual old-fashioned photographs or pictures from a home printer. The better quality of paper you use, the nicer your ornaments will look. When you've got all your pictures ready, cut them to fit the wood slices. The easiest way to do this is to simply set a wood slice down on the picture you want to use and then draw around the wood slice with a pencil. Cut out the picture, then glue it onto the wood slice, being careful not to let any bubbles form under the picture. (A credit card used as a squeegee will get rid of any bubbles!)

Once the glue dries, finish the ornament with some sort of sealant. Craft glues such as Mod Podge will both seal your photos and glue them onto your wood slices, or you can use a paint sealant and wood glue. Whatever you do, you'll want to place some sort of seal over your photos and the back of your ornament. This will stop the wood from rotting and keep your pictures from yellowing or peeling off the wood.

After the sealant dries, drill a small hole into the top of the ornament and run a ribbon through the hole for easy hanging. When hanging your ornaments on your Remembrance Tree, you'll have to tie them onto the cage, so use a loose knot so they can be easily untied when putting them away later. Alternatively, you can run an ornament hook or paper clip through the hole in the ornament and then simply hang it on the tree.

Using Your Remembrance Tree

When I set up my Remembrance Tree each year in late November, I say the name of each person who is on an ornament and invite them to continue to be a part of my Yuletide celebrations. When I take down my tree, I say their names yet again and thank them for being a part of the year's festivities. I believe that saying the names of our beloved dead is vitally important for preserving their memory and keeping them close to our hearts.

I place a star on the top of my Remembrance Tree (the kind designed for the top of a regular Christmas tree) to serve as a guidepost to my home for those I've lost. When placing the star on top of my tree, I say:

May the light symbolized by this star bring those I love back to me and let them know I still care.

Providing offerings of food and drink to our beloved dead is a standard practice in my spiritual traditions. Luckily, a Remembrance Tree provides a wonderful opportunity to engage in such things. At large holiday meals or gatherings, fix a plate for those you've lost and place it near your tree (or even under the tree if the tomato cage you're using is large enough) for their enjoyment. The dead don't "eat" food like you or I do, but instead take in the essence of the food and utilize it. Within twenty-four hours of your offering, dispose of what you've given to the dead either outside, in the compost bin, or in the garbage. (Just be sure not to eat the offering. It's considered bad manners and might also bring some bad luck!)

I'm a big fan of leaving liquid libations near my Remembrance Tree, even more so than food. It's easy enough to pour those I've lost a glass of wine or a dram of whiskey if I'm celebrating with friends, and even the dead want a little wassail! Alcohol is a wonderful offering because it evaporates rather quickly and doesn't require any cleanup.

When adding a new individual to my Remembrance Tree, I like to do a little ceremony to honor them instead of just putting their ornament on my tree. The words aren't especially important, but I usually say something similar to this:

> *(Name of person), though you are no longer here with me in the flesh, I know that you are still a part of my life. The holidays are for friends and family, and though we*

are now separated, you will always be among my beloveds. I place this ornament upon my Remembrance Tree in honor of you, and as long as it hangs from this tree, you will be a part of my Yuletide celebrations. Though I grieve your passing, you are cherished, you are honored, and you are forever in my heart and the hearts of everyone who continues to love you. Be welcome!

I like to keep my Remembrance Tree in a place where it won't be disturbed but can be seen on a regular basis. In my house, this usually means a decorative corner of the kitchen, away from the prying eyes of guests but visible to my wife and me as we go about our holiday work. What is remembered lives!

The End of Yuletide

For most of us today, New Year's Day marks the end of the Yule season. Those of us with a deep and obsessive love for the holidays might try to make the season last until Three Kings' Day or even Plough Monday, but despite our yearning for a longer season, it does eventually come to an end. By January 7, most of the Yuletide decorations at my house have been taken down and the festive energy of the winter holiday season begins to recede. I don't shed any tears while packing up a lifetime's worth of Yule decorations every January, but it's a task that's always accompanied by a touch of melancholy.

Many of my friends tease me about keeping my Yuletide decorations up past New Year's, but there's a lot of precedent for it. In medieval Europe, decorations often stayed up until the first of February. Today it's generally considered unlucky to leave decorations up past Twelfth Day, so it's best not to procrastinate too much.

As I pack up my holiday treasures every January, I can't help but perform one more act of Yuletide magic. As I lovingly place stockings, candles, Yule logs, and other miscellanea in large red and green plastic tubs, I say the following blessing as I place the lids on my bins:

With joy we celebrated the holiday,
And now we pack our mementos away.
Gifts we have received and gifts we have given,
Tales of sun, child, and Claus to all who would listen.
Twinkling lights, fire in the hearth, and candles bright,
All to drive away the darkness of the night.
May we remember the magic, laughter, and cheer,
And be with those we love at Yule again next year!

CONCLUSION

Yuletide is one of our oldest and most cherished holiday seasons. It's embraced by billions of people every year across the religious spectrum. It's a season for personal reflection, riotous celebrations, time with family, and sharing the very best of ourselves with those around us. The light of Yuletide has been with us for over 2,500 years and is brighter than ever today.

I believe that Yuletide is the most magical season of all. Yule encourages us to embrace our inner child, to believe in Santa, Befana, and the Krampus. It's a season of wonder and a time to contemplate divine beginnings and magical stars. Yuletide is also subversive: a time to be things we generally are not, to celebrate Christmas poopers, and to embrace the freedom that comes with self-indulgent partying.

As you celebrate Yuletide, find time every year to really take it all in. Notice the various religious and spiritual observances going on around you. When at the mall, feel the chaotic energy of the season and find strength in it. Let the decorations and traditions of your family connect you with those you've lost and remind you of previous holiday celebrations.

And for those who truly love the spirit of the Yuletide season, never forget that it echoes throughout the year as the seasons change. In the spring, there's always that one forgotten or lost decoration that appears when tidying up the living room. By August, many craft stores have started putting out holiday items. As autumn begins, colder nights and shorter days whisper to us that Yuletide is fast approaching. Halloween costumes and trick-or-treating bring to mind Misrule and wassails past, and let us know that Yuletide is almost nigh once more ... and then the holidays begin again! No matter how you celebrate, I wish you and yours a joyous Yuletide, the most magical season of them all!

ACKNOWLEDGMENTS

Thanks to my wife, Ari, for always treating my Yule obsession with patience and grace. My father has made Yuletide special for over forty years now. All of those Christmases past were definitely appreciated! To my grandparents, Mick and Marie, whose house was always a holiday wonderland to me as a child, my goal every December is to recreate the magic you so happily shared with everyone.

Thanks to everyone at Llewellyn for being enthusiastic when I first suggested this project, most especially my editors Elysia Gallo and Andrea Neff. They really do make everything they touch better! To my brothers, Chuck, Dason, and Derick, thanks for sharing some of the most magical days of my life with me. And finally, to my friend Mickie Mueller, your *Little Book of Halloween* was the inspiration for this book. I'm much appreciative (and you are awesome).

BIBLIOGRAPHY

I have been obsessed with the holidays since elementary school, and have read everything I've been able to get my hands on about the holidays ever since! What follows are some of my favorite books on the season, and the ones I found myself using most often to look up the stray fact or four.

Bowler, Gerry. *Christmas in the Crosshairs.* New York: Oxford University Press, 2017.

———. *Santa Claus: A Biography.* Toronto: McClelland & Stewart, 2007. Bowler skips a lot of the evidence relating Odin to Santa Claus, but his exploration of Santa's last two hundred years is a tour de force.

———. *The World Encyclopedia of Christmas.* Toronto: McClelland & Stewart, 2000. Bowler is the most prolific writer working in the Christmas genre today.

Cater, Colin, and Karen Cater. *Wassailing: Reawakening an Ancient Folk Custom.* Hedingham, Essex, UK: Hedingham Fair, 2013. What a fabulous book! Chock-full of English history and folk traditions.

Forbes, Bruce David. *Christmas: A Candid History.* Berkeley, CA: University of California Press, 2007. Forbes writes about the holidays honestly, stripping away most of the Christian whitewash that has been added to them over the centuries. Despite being published by an academic press, this is a concise and easily readable book about the origins of Christmas. The material here was also republished in Forbes's *America's Favorite Holidays: Candid Histories* in 2015.

Hutton, Ronald. *Stations of the Sun: A History of the Ritual Year in Britain.* New York: Oxford University Press, 1996. Paperback edition, 1997. *Stations of the Sun* is the most dog-eared book in my personal library. There's great information on nearly every page!

Nissenbaum, Stephen. *The Battle for Christmas: A Cultural History of America's Most Cherished Holiday.* New York: Vintage Books, 1997. Nissenbaum's book is a far-ranging one, and one of the most honest accountings of the December holidays I've ever come across.

Raedisch, Linda. *The Old Magic of Christmas: Yuletide Traditions for the Darkest Days of the Year.* Woodbury, MN: Llewellyn Publications, 2013. For those interested in a scarier Yuletide, Raedisch's book is essential reading.

Shaw, Philip A. *Pagan Goddesses in the Early Germanic World: Eostre, Hreda, and the Cult of Matrons,* London: Bristol Classical Press, 2011. Shaw spends some time writing about Bede and the Anglo-Saxon celebration of Mother's Night.